T0293992

THE CSIRO gut CARE GUIDE

Pan Macmillan Australia

THE CSIRO gut CARE GUIDE

FOREWORD BY
DR ROSEMARY STANTON OAM

We've come a long way in discussing the part of the body between the mouth and the anus. For a start, we can now call it the 'gut', a word that once provoked some indignation when uttered by a child. We have also discovered the immense value of dietary fibre and stopped dismissing it as mere 'roughage'. Although we're not quite there yet, many of us are also happy to use the word 'fart', and hopefully will soon recognise it as a sign of a healthy microbiome!

The old idea that dietary fibre is a single substance has almost gone. Most people realise that terms such as vitamins and minerals embrace many different substances. We now need to understand that dietary fibre includes a wide range of compounds, found in a diverse range of plant foods. And just as consuming lots of one particular vitamin won't meet your needs for the other 12, no single type of dietary fibre will fulfil all the body's needs.

For centuries, interest in dietary fibre was confined mainly to its effects on laxation. In the 6th century BC, Hippocrates exhorted his followers to eat bran. The Reverend Sylvester Graham, an early health-food crusader in North America, gave his name to a wholewheat cracker to assist laxation. Britain's Dr Thomas Allinson similarly preached the virtues of a special wholemeal loaf – and was barred from practising as a doctor as a result. Switzerland's Dr Bircher-Benner stretched the idea by combining fresh fruit with oats for his famous Bircher muesli. More recently, Drs Trowell and Burkitt noticed that indigenous Africans ate large amounts of dietary fibre, passed large stools and had few bowel problems while the English ate fine white bread, had small stools and a high incidence of bowel problems. I remember interviewing Dr Burkitt on TV as he travelled the world, preaching his high-fibre story.

The world's first International Conference on Dietary Fibre in 1982 in New Zealand was possibly the best conference I ever attended. Some of the world's notable professors of medicine left lectures with their pockets bulging with slices of Vogel's bread from an exhibitor – possibly the only source of dietary fibre in the food provided by the conference organisers. I also remember Professor Mark Wahlqvist, one of the most notable and far-sighted Australian nutritionists, asking us all to consider not only the many types of dietary fibre but also the company they kept. The foods naturally rich in different types of dietary fibre also provide us with vitamins, minerals and a vast range of protective phytonutrients. Foods high in added sugars, poor-quality fats, preservatives, colourings, flavourings and other additives are usually poor sources of dietary fibre.

However, the greatest fillip to the dietary fibre saga has been the gut microbiome. A healthy gut microbiome thrives on a diverse diet rich in healthy high-fibre foods. A good reason to forget fad diets that omit whole classes of plant foods.

Our task now is to understand the importance of the gut microbiome. And here to help is *The CSIRO Gut Care Guide*. The timing is perfect.

Dr Rosemary Stanton OAM

 Our task now is to understand the importance of the gut microbiome. And here to help is *The CSIRO Gut Care Guide*. The timing is perfect.

CONTENTS

ABOUT THE AUTHORS

Dr Michael Conlon

Michael is a principal research scientist at CSIRO Health and Biosecurity, with a PhD in biochemistry from the University of Adelaide. Dr Conlon has more than 30 years' experience in investigating the impact of foods and diets on physiological processes and health outcomes through preclinical and clinical research trials. A focus of his work has been on understanding the effects of dietary components such as fibre, resistant starch, proteins and oils on gut physiology, as well as other tissues and systems of the body. Michael's work has also involved investigating the roles of microbes, such as bacteria, in mediating the effects of diet on the large bowel, including studies to examine and develop prebiotic fibres and probiotics. He has shown that the inclusion of resistant starch and fibres in the diet can help protect against the toxic effects of poor-quality 'Western' diets on the large bowel, demonstrating that resistant starch can reduce the risk of tissue damage that may contribute to serious colorectal diseases. Michael's vast body of research has also demonstrated the important role of fermentation by gut microbes in producing short-chain fatty acids, which help to maintain a healthy environment within the large bowel. Michael has continued to apply his research to understanding and helping prevent adverse health conditions such as inflammatory bowel disease and colorectal cancer. Michael also has a keen interest in developing new foods and nutraceuticals with gut health applications.

Dr Pennie Taylor

Pennie is a research scientist and clinical dietitian at CSIRO Health and Biosecurity and holds a PhD through the University of Adelaide's School of Medicine, exploring dietary strategies to optimise glucose variability and self-management using real-time continuous glucose monitoring for individuals with type 2 diabetes. With over 15 years' experience in clinical practice and nutrition research, Pennie's research focuses on how digital health technologies and dietary patterns can support weight management, including weight-loss surgery, and help prevent chronic and clinical disease. At the CSIRO, her diverse skills cover development and delivery of large complex clinical and community trials that explore the influence of food components and dietary composition on health outcomes. Pennie extends these skills working with industry partners to translate scientific research into food and nutrition solutions, including developing foods and digital lifestyle programs. Pennie co-authors *The CSIRO Healthy Gut Diet* and *The CSIRO Low-carb Diet* book series, which were recently translated into commercially available ready-made meals designed to comply with the CSIRO Low-carb Diet. As a practising dietitian, Pennie remains an active member of the primary health community and is an active committee member for the Australian and New Zealand Metabolic and Obesity Surgery Society (ANZMOSS) and the American Society of Metabolic and Bariatric Surgery (ASMBS) and a member of the Primary Health Network Clinical Council.

Dr Cuong D Tran

Cuong is a senior research scientist at CSIRO Health and Biosecurity. Cuong is also an affiliate senior lecturer at the University of Adelaide. Cuong has a PhD in nutritional physiology and gastroenterology, and more than 15 years of research experience in gut health and nutrition, as well as gut disorders and wellbeing in children and adults. Prior to completing his PhD in 2001, Cuong worked for an industry company looking at novel therapies for eradicating *Helicobacter pylori* infection, also working in the Gastroenterology Unit at the Women's and Children's Hospital, investigating *H. pylori* eradication. In 2003, Cuong did his postdoctoral training at the University of Colorado Health Sciences Centre in Denver, after being awarded the Inaugural American Australian Association Fellowship. Returning to Australia with an National Health and Medical Research Council industry fellowship working at the Women's and Children's Hospital in Adelaide. Cuong's research investigated zinc in combination with other nutraceuticals in the treatment of *H. pylori* infection. Following this, Cuong focused on establishing a micronutrient therapy laboratory based on his research into micronutrients and gastrointestinal diseases. In 2011, Cuong was made Senior Research Fellow at the Women's and Children's Health Network, investigating the role of zinc nutrition in children with gastroenterological diseases. Since 2013, Cuong has been with the CSIRO, researching how different diet and lifestyle components may modulate gut and metabolic health and intestinal permeability. With a strong interest in gut-barrier function and the microbiome, and how these impact health and wellbeing, and in developing effective measures of gut health and function, Cuong has published over 50 peer-reviewed papers on topics, such as the gut microbiome and health, zinc nutrition as a potential therapy for inflammatory gut conditions, non-invasive testing for gut health, and small bowel integrity and function. Cuong is currently working on commercialising a gut-health test and nutritional solutions to improve population gut health and wellbeing.

Megan Rebuli

Megan is an experienced research dietitian and nutritionist with CSIRO Health and Biosecurity. Megan has a background in public health nutrition, community nutrition programs, and dietary assessment and treatment in practice. Megan's research experience focuses on the relationship between nutrition and health, and how changing dietary behaviour can improve health outcomes. She works across a range of areas including the design of nutrition programs, delivery of clinical nutrition trials, application of digital programs in dietary interventions, and the development of tools to assess dietary intake and analyse dietary patterns. Megan understands Australians' food preferences and uses this knowledge to adapt recipes and to share practical skills for a healthy diet. Megan contributed to *The CSIRO Healthy Gut Diet*, *The CSIRO Low-carb Diet* and the commercially available ready meals, and the CSIRO Healthy Diet Score. Megan is passionate about good food, good science, and bringing it all together.

The CSIRO, Australia's national science agency, has been dedicated to the practical application of knowledge and science for society and industry since 1928. Today the CSIRO ranks in the top 1 per cent of world scientific institutions in 12 out of 22 research fields. CSIRO Health and Biosecurity conducts research into human health, including disease prevention, diagnosis and innovative treatment solutions.

As Australia's national science agency, we solve the greatest challenges through innovative science and technology.

We are thinkers, problem solvers, leaders. We blaze new trails of discovery. We aim to inspire the next generation.

We collaborate with industry, government, universities and research organisations to turn big ideas into disruptive solutions.

We use collaborative research to turn science into solutions for food security and quality; clean energy and resources; health and wellbeing; resilient and valuable environments; innovative industries; and a secure Australia and region.

We are unlocking a better future. We are CSIRO.

INTRODUCTION

Most of us are aware that the gut plays a major role in our overall wellbeing. However, you may be surprised by just *how* important it is – at every stage of life.

Over the years, we've come to understand more about the gut and, in particular, about the huge collection of bacteria – the gut microbiome – that it sustains, and their role in helping to develop and maintain a healthy metabolism, a healthy brain and a healthy immune system. We now also know that a major piece in the gut health puzzle is fibre, especially a type of dietary fibre called resistant starch.

As we've unravelled the interactions between our gut microbiome and our immune system, we've learned that this all starts at birth, when microbial colonisation of the gut occurs. This early microbiome has a role in shaping the development of a person's immune system. Eating the right types of foods for feeding the gut microbiome during infancy has been shown to have life-long immune-system benefits.

By the age of about two-and-a-half to four years, the gut microbiome has fully developed. The make-up of the microbiome population of an individual then remains relatively stable throughout adulthood, although significant alterations can occur. There are also gradual shifts as we age. Establishing a good gut microbiome early on plays an important role in maintaining health throughout life.

An imbalance in our gut microbiome – microbial dysbiosis – can be brought on by poor diet and lifestyle choices over the long term, including a diet low in dietary fibre and high in processed foods. It may contribute to the development of disease, including type 2 diabetes. Individual differences in the composition of our gut microbiome may affect how the body reacts to some dietary components and may also predispose some people to particular diseases. Advances in analysing our microbiome may help deepen our understanding of its role in human health, and allow us to personalise diets to improve our health and wellbeing.

We now know that a major piece in the gut health puzzle is fibre, especially a type of dietary fibre called resistant starch.

HOW TO USE THIS BOOK

Since the publication of *The CSIRO Healthy Gut Diet* book in 2017, we have received many enquiries from Australians of all ages, seeking further information as well as tips to improve their gut health. In this book, we provide an update on the latest science and look at how the gut changes over time. We also share some new recipes to encourage you to add dietary fibre to your meals in simple and delicious ways.

You'll also find a range of helpful tips and quick meal-building solutions commonly used by dietitians, and simple daily meal plans, suitable for families, shift-workers and those preparing meals for one.

When it comes to nutritional science, there are always new and emerging discoveries. This book is an extension of *The CSIRO Healthy Gut Diet* plan and is designed to provide you with the latest updates on the evidence surrounding nutrition and gut health, in a meaningful and practical way.

1

In **Part One**, we describe how the gut works in harmony with the microbiome to promote wellbeing, explaining the science behind the CSIRO Healthy Gut Diet. We look at the gut at different stages of life, and talk about fibre, as well as other dietary components that have a role in shaping our gut.

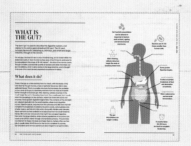

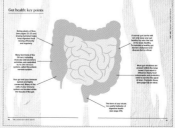

2

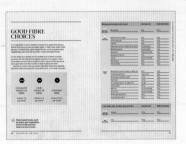

In **Part Two**, we outline the CSIRO Healthy Gut Eating Plan and list foods rich in fibre and resistant starch. In this section, you'll also find a daily food guide, tips and sample meal plans to show how you can reach your recommended fibre target in an easy and appetising way.

3

In **Part Three**, you'll find 60 fibre-fuelled recipes that tie in with the CSIRO Healthy Gut Eating Plan. These recipes are designed to deliver a range of different fibres, including resistant starch, using a variety of wholefoods to also provide a balance of essential vitamins and nutrients.

PART ONE

THE
gut
AND OUR
HEALTH

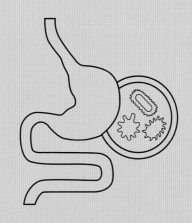

WHAT IS THE GUT?

The term 'gut' is used to describe the digestive system, and relates to the entire gastrointestinal (GI) tract. The GI tract includes the mouth, oesophagus, stomach, and small and large intestine, through to the rectum.

On average, the total GI tract is about 9 metres long, and is folded within the abdominal cavity. In fact, the total surface area of the GI tract is estimated to be somewhere in the range of 30–40 metres^2 – the size of two tennis courts. The gut contains a substantial quantity of bacteria and other microbes: our gut microbiome, which mainly resides in the large intestine, and is thought to be one of the most densely populated ecosystems in nature.

What does it do?

Think of the gut as a tube starting from the mouth, with the inside of the tube lined by the gut mucosa, a type of epthelial tissue (our skin is also epithelial tissue). This is a complex structure that increases the available surface area of the gut for absorbing nutrients from our food as it travels further through to the lower gut. After chewing, salivary enzymes in the mouth begin the work of breaking down food. Once swallowed, food travels down the oesophagus to the stomach, where it is mixed with acids and enzymes. Some protein digestion begins here. The contents of the stomach are released gradually into the small intestine, where most digestion occurs. Digestive juices, enzymes from the pancreas and bile from the liver complete the breakdown of proteins into amino acids, carbohydrates into simpler sugars, and fats into fatty acids. Along with vitamins and minerals, these nutrients are then available to be absorbed from the small intestine. Dietary fibre and any components that might have escaped digestion then enter the large intestine, where diverse populations of microbes can break some of them down through a fermentation process. This provides nourishment for these microbes and helps them to multiply. After our first bite, it usually takes 24–60 hours for the food to complete its journey. Our circulatory and nervous systems are also integral to our gut function.

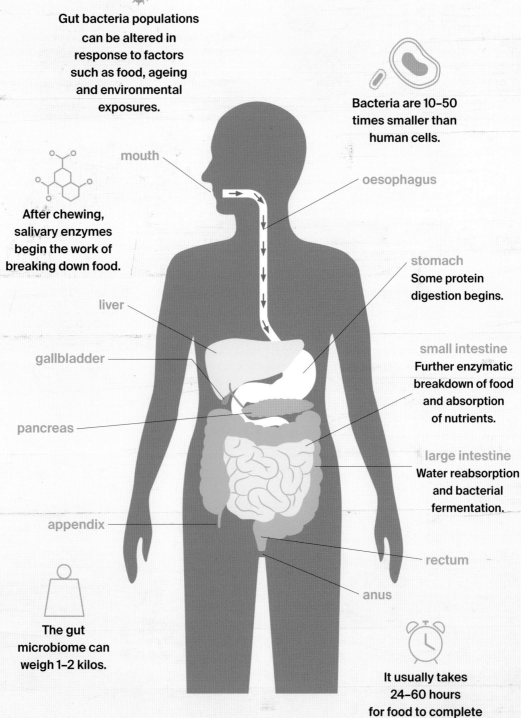

Gut bacteria populations can be altered in response to factors such as food, ageing and environmental exposures.

Bacteria are 10–50 times smaller than human cells.

After chewing, salivary enzymes begin the work of breaking down food.

mouth

oesophagus

stomach
Some protein digestion begins.

liver

small intestine
Further enzymatic breakdown of food and absorption of nutrients.

gallbladder

pancreas

large intestine
Water reabsorption and bacterial fermentation.

appendix

rectum

anus

The gut microbiome can weigh 1–2 kilos.

It usually takes 24–60 hours for food to complete its journey.

THE ESSENTIAL ROLE OF FIBRE

Dietary fibre consists of a diverse group of mostly plant-based complex carbohydrates that are not digested – that is, they are not broken down by the enzymes in the upper gastrointestinal tract.

Since dietary fibres are not digested in the small intestine, they are available as a food source for the gut microbiome populations that abound in the large intestine.

Of the nutrients we consume, fibre has the biggest influence on the gut microbiome. A diverse range of dietary fibres creates a diverse and more resilient gut microbiome, leading to good gut health by building an environment less favourable to the growth of potentially harmful microbes, while also enhancing the immune system and the healthy functioning of the tissues and gut barrier (see page 42).

A healthy gut environment is associated with a decreased risk of a range of diseases, including bowel cancer, type 2 diabetes and obesity.

Fibres are generally classified as soluble or insoluble. On pages 22–27, we take you through the key functions of soluble and insoluble fibres, as well as resistant starch, and share the best food sources for a diverse intake of fibre.

 A healthy gut environment is associated with a decreased risk of a range of diseases, including bowel cancer, type 2 diabetes and obesity.

Soluble fibres

Soluble fibres dissolve in water to form viscous gels that slow the passage of ingested food through the upper gastrointestinal tract. Soluble fibres are also rapidly and extensively fermented in the large intestine, making them a good source of fuel for your gut bacteria.

Key functions

Soluble fibres:

* are important for general health, as they help to lower cholesterol and slow blood glucose uptake;

* slow digestion, which helps control hunger and increases the body's ability to absorb beneficial nutrients;

* support the growth and activity of beneficial bacteria.

Soluble fibres are fermented in the large intestine, supporting the growth of beneficial gut bacteria.

**Nuts, seeds
and legumes.**

Oats, barley and
psyllium husk.

BEST
SOURCES OF
soluble
fibres

Fruit
including apples,
mango, pears,
oranges and
prunes.

Most vegetables,
but especially brussels
sprouts, eggplant, peas,
broad beans, green
beans, parsnips, okra
and onion.

Insoluble fibres

Previously called roughage, insoluble fibres account for about 70 per cent of most plant-food fibre. They tend to be slowly and incompletely fermented by the gut, commonly increasing stool bulk. Some insoluble fibres are fermented, helping to increase beneficial bacteria.

Key functions

Insoluble fibres:

* attract and retain water, increasing the volume of food and creating a sense of fullness to control appetite

* assist in propelling food along the gastrointestinal tract

* increase stool bulk and aid in laxation.

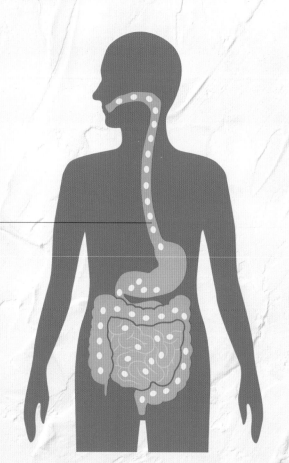

Insoluble fibres help to propel your food along the gastrointestinal tract.

Legumes, such as chickpeas, beans, lentils and split peas.

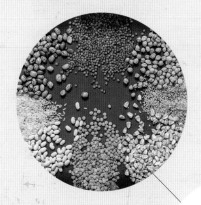

Most wholegrain foods, such as cereals, bread and pasta.

BEST SOURCES OF
insoluble fibres

Nuts and **seeds**.

Most vegetables, but especially peas and green beans, spinach, silverbeet, cabbage, broccoli, beetroot, parsnip, carrot and brussels sprouts.

Most fruit, but especially unpeeled pears and apples, oranges, passionfruit, figs, strawberries and raspberries.

Resistant starch

Resistant starch is also classified as dietary fibre. It is starch that resists digestion in the small intestine, and thereby passes through to the large intestine, where it is used by the gut microbiome. Although resistant starch is an insoluble fibre, it is extensively fermented by the gut microbiome.

Butyrate, and other short-chain fatty acids such as acetate and propionate, are beneficial by-products of this fermentation. Butyrate is especially important as it plays an important role in protecting our gut wall. It also helps with digestion and optimises immune function.

Resistant starch is available in starchy foods, often in small amounts, and uniquely it can be formed during food preparation and production. An example of this is the starch in potatoes, and how it changes when it is cooked, then chilled, before eating. This heating and cooling effect changes the structure of the starch, making it more resistant to digestion – leading to a modest rise in the resistant starch content of the potato.

Key functions

Resistant starch:

* encourages the growth and activity of beneficial bacteria, especially those producing butyrate – a short-chain fatty acid that is a health-promoting fuel for bacteria in the large intestine

* helps to lower cholesterol and assists with blood glucose control.

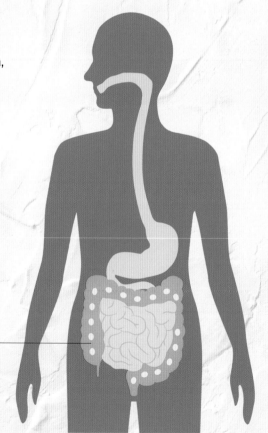

Resistant starch is fermented in the large intestine, creating bowel-protective by-products including butyrate.

Legumes, especially chickpeas.

Grains, including rye, buckwheat, millet, oats and barley.

BEST SOURCES OF
resistant starch

Cooled, cooked starchy foods, such as potatoes, sweet potatoes, rice, pasta and beans.

Under-ripe bananas and green banana starch.

Novel cereals, such as those containing the BARLEYmax™ grains, high-amylose wheat and high-amylose maize.

Fibre and our gut microbes

Gut microbes play a crucial role in maintaining our health. Most of the microbes in our GI tract can be found within the large intestine. They help provide the body with many essential micronutrients, such as vitamin K and some of the B complex vitamins, and generate many other compounds, including short-chain fatty acids such as butyrate (see page 26).

Butyrate acts as the primary energy source for the cells lining the large intestine, and also has many other benefits, including for the immune system. A diet with plenty of dietary fibre will provide microbes with the fuel they need for these important functions.

Many hundreds of different types of bacteria and other microbes (yeasts, for example) can be present within the human gut; the exact combination of bacterial types varies between individuals. As the requirements for growth for each of these microbes often differs, eating an array of dietary fibres (see pages 22–27) and other nutrients will help maintain the growth of a diverse range of bacteria.

Dietary fibres generally promote the growth of beneficial bacteria, and this helps to reduce the chances of harmful bacteria gaining a foothold. A diet low in fibre, as well as other influences, such as disease, infection and antibiotic use, can lead to adverse shifts in gut microbe populations: this imbalance is known as dysbiosis.

THE IMPORTANCE OF FIBRE DIVERSITY

Since the various types of fibres mentioned throughout this book vary in their capacity to promote gut health and function, the best option is to consume a wide variety of wholefoods that are as close to their natural state as possible – wholegrains, fruits, vegetables, legumes, nuts and seeds – as this will provide a variety of fibre in our diet. Consuming a diversity of fibres ensures that a diverse range of beneficial gut microbial species can thrive and thereby promote gut health.

✳ Consuming a
diversity of fibres
ensures that a
diverse range
of beneficial gut
microbial species
can thrive.

How much fibre do we need?

The recommended total daily fibre intake in Australia is 25 grams for women and 30 grams for men. These amounts are considered adequate for maintaining gut function and laxation. However, to reduce the risk of chronic diseases, the National Health and Medical Research Council suggests a higher daily intake of 28 grams for women and 38 grams for men.

The meal plans on pages 110–117 show how easy it is to reach your recommended daily fibre targets, whatever your lifestyle.

Recommended total daily fibre intake:

*25 g   *30 g

WOMEN   MEN

MICROBES, FERMENTATION AND GAS

Fermentation is the process by which microbes act on food components reaching the large intestine, breaking them down to release other components that can then be used by the body – or to reduce components that can be toxic.

This microbe-mediated fermentation activity, which occurs in oxygen-depleted environments, is similar to that which occurs when creating fermented foods (see pages 56–57). A common by-product of fermentation is gas.

A diet containing fibre, especially soluble fibres and resistant starch, will lead to greater fermentation – and hence more gas production – in the lower GI tract. This is an unavoidable and normal part of consuming fibre-rich foods.

Can we have too much fibre?

Understanding how your body responds to an increasing amount of fibre is important, as this will allow you to identify how much you can tolerate. If you are not used to having much fibre in your diet, a sudden increase may sometimes produce abdominal discomfort and increased flatulence (gas).

Here are some simple ways to minimise these side effects:

* Start slowly, by increasing your fibre intake gradually over a week.

* Spread your consumption of high-fibre foods throughout the day (don't just eat them at breakfast, for example).

* Maintain or begin physical activity – even walking is a great start to help your gut muscles contract and function more effectively.

* Drink plenty of water to complement your exercise activities. Fibre needs water to help move it along!

Foods high in dietary fibre are often bulky. When consumed as part of a whole food diet and at regular times throughout the day, these foods can make you feel quite full, making it difficult to over-eat dietary fibre. A diet low in dietary fibre is the most common reason for constipation.

Please note that some individuals may require low fibre or reduced types of fibre to help manage health conditions. If this is you, please speak to your healthcare professional for guidance on how to adapt your fibre intake appropriately.

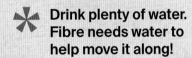

Drink plenty of water. Fibre needs water to help move it along!

THE IMPORTANCE OF GUT HEALTH

As well as being an organ of digestion and nutrient absorption, the gastrointestinal tract serves as a physical and biochemical interface between our internal and external environments. This vital nexus is known as the gut barrier.

How the gut changes as we travel through life

There is growing recognition that as we travel through life, diet – in particular the macronutrients we consume – has a major role in shaping the health of our gut. Our gut health is also strongly influenced by environmental factors and lifestyle choices.

Birth

How a baby is born is the first major contributor to its gut microbiome. Babies born naturally are first colonised by microbes from their mother's birth canal, and often the mother's faecal microbiome, as well as through her mammary glands during breastfeeding, along with microbes present on the mother's skin and mouth, and in the immediate environment. Studies have shown that the gut microbiomes of babies born by Caesarean section have a less diverse gut microbiome in early infancy, compared to those delivered vaginally, and this can increase their susceptibility to infections and gut issues. This has led to a practice known as vaginal seeding, where babies born by C-section are swabbed with a sample of their mother's vaginal microbiome. While vaginal seeding has been shown to help support the development of the microbiome in the short term, the long-term effects are unknown.

Infancy

During the first months of life, newborns are vulnerable to disease, as their immune system has not developed, and the mucosal lining, or epithelium, in their small intestine is anatomically and functionally immature. Their gut barrier isn't fully formed, making it more open, or 'permeable', and allowing more things to pass through it. During infancy, this gut permeability can have beneficial effects, such as enhanced uptake of nutrients. However, it also leaves the body more susceptible to microbes and foreign particles, leading to infection and inflammation.

It is likely that growth factors, hormones, breast milk and the composition of the gut microbiome all facilitate growth of the gut.

During the first year of life, milk (especially breastmilk) is considered the optimal food source for growing infants. The gradual introduction of a wide range of foods during weaning promotes a shift in the gut microbiome towards that seen in healthy adults. Other environmental factors, plus exposure to antibiotics and infection, also play a major role in determining the distinctive characteristics of the microbial community in an infant's gut.

In general, over the first two years of life, an infant's gut microbiome begins to resemble that of an adult's. By the time infants are about two-and-a-half to four years of age, their gut microbiome has fully matured.

Developing a stable core of diverse gut microbiome species early in life is critical and advantageous for maintaining health.

> **Over the first two years of life, the infant's gut begins to resemble that of an adult's.**

Adulthood

Maintaining a diverse gut microbiome is positively correlated with good gut health. Microbiome diversity can be temporarily affected by changes in diet, sickness and other lifestyle factors during adulthood (see pages 46–47).

Mature age

In our later years, the composition of the gut microbiome often becomes less diverse, and gut 'leakiness' may increase.

Lifestyle factors, including diet and exercise, as well as genetic and environmental factors (pollutants, poor sanitation), may all contribute to the decline in diversity of our gut microbiome. Extended use of antibiotics can also have a detrimental impact on the composition of the gut microbiome.

As we advance in age, we are at greater risk of disorders such as irritable bowel syndrome, inflammatory bowel diseases, coeliac disease and colorectal cancer – these are often linked with shifts in our gut microbiome.

ETHNICITY AND COUNTRY OF BIRTH

Our genetics and ethnic background, country of birth and where we've spent time living, as well as our socio-economic status, may influence the microbes and functioning of our gut. Cultural differences – especially in the type and variety of foods consumed – can influence our microbe populations and their activities. How these microbe populations become entrenched by long-term dietary patterns is still unclear.

Our genetics and ethnic origins can influence our ability to digest or metabolise foods. For example, it is quite common for people in some Asian countries to find it more difficult to break down alcohol, because they have inherited a deficiency in an enzyme involved in the process. Similarly, after weaning, many people lack the ability to efficiently break down lactose, a sugar found in milk from cows, goats, sheep and camels. This can cause significant gut discomfort, and is more prevalent in people from Africa, Asia and South America.

Different food practices, as well as the differences in the types of food that grow in a region, significantly influence our diet, and therefore potentially influence our health. Unfortunately, many people in countries such as Australia consume typical 'Western' diets, which are high in saturated fats, protein (including processed meats) and foods with added sugars and salt, while lacking the dietary fibres and other beneficial compounds found in plant foods, which are needed to maintain good digestive health.

 Our genetics and ethnic origins can influence our ability to digest or metabolise foods.

The gut microbiome across the lifespan

In early life, maternal and environmental factors shape the development of the gut microbiome communities (less diverse) and the gut barrier (a leakier gut). The gut is colonised with bacteria and diversity develops throughout infancy and early childhood, with a subsequent decrease of the initially high intestinal permeability as the gut matures. In the early life stages, factors such

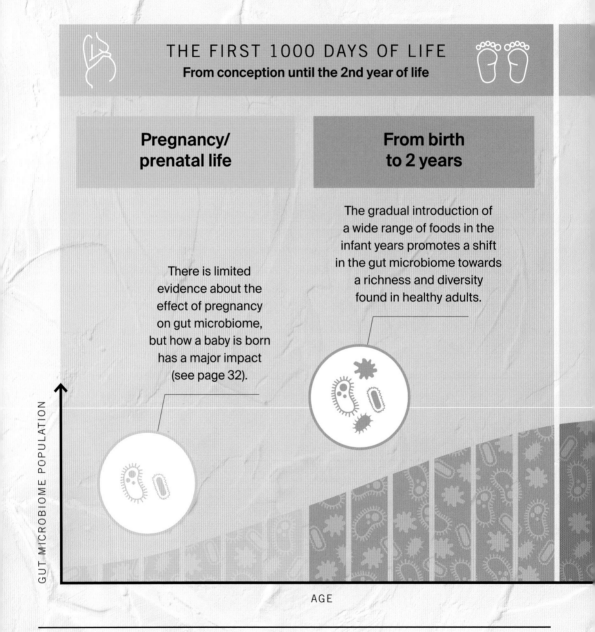

THE FIRST 1000 DAYS OF LIFE
From conception until the 2nd year of life

Pregnancy/ prenatal life

From birth to 2 years

The gradual introduction of a wide range of foods in the infant years promotes a shift in the gut microbiome towards a richness and diversity found in healthy adults.

There is limited evidence about the effect of pregnancy on gut microbiome, but how a baby is born has a major impact (see page 32).

GUT MICROBIOME POPULATION

AGE

as delivery mode, breastfeeding, nutrition, antibiotics and increased intestinal permeability can influence the development of a diverse gut microbiome population. The gut microbiome in a young child (between two-and-a-half to four years old) starts to resemble that of a young adult.

In adulthood, events in early life combine with tight intestinal permeability to influence the healthy adult gut microbiome, which remains stable throughout much of adult life. This is positively associated with good health outcomes. In later adulthood years, the diversity of the gut microbiome declines, and gut leakiness increases. This low diversity and changes in leakiness can lead to an increased risk of developing chronic diseases.

ADULTHOOD

MATURE AGE

The microbiome is quite stable but can be temporarily affected by diet, illness and other lifestyle factors.

In our later years, there is lower diversity and gut leakiness may increase.

AGE

Gut health and the rest of the body

This section looks at several important interactions or linkages between the gut and the rest of the body, and how the activities of the gut – especially the activities and products of gut microbes – can potentially influence the tissues of the rest of the body (and in some instances, vice versa).

The means by which different organs and tissues are connected to the gut are often not clearly understood, but the transfer of nutrients, toxins, inflammatory substances or hormones via the circulatory system (both vascular and lymphatic) are the likely mechanisms. Signalling via the nervous system, or the movement of immune cells between the tissues, may also facilitate connections.

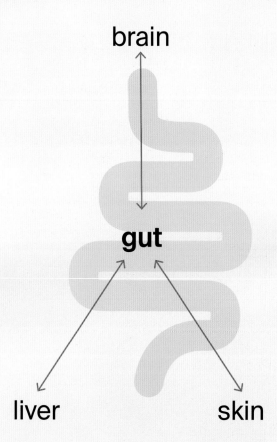

brain

gut

liver   skin

1 The gut–brain axis

The gut and the brain constantly interact, with signals being sent in both directions, via nerves and hormones. These signals enable actions and communications about the digestion process, substances present in the gut, and whether our energy stores are running low. There is mounting evidence that products of the many microbes in the gut can reach or influence the brain, and even affect our mood and anxiety levels.

2 The gut–liver axis

Blood is delivered to the liver from the gastrointestinal tract via the hepatic portal vein; the liver then metabolises or detoxifies the substances it receives, making them safe and usable for the tissues of the body. This includes absorbed nutrients from food, as well as the products of microbes. The foods we eat, our gut microbes and our gut physiology all play a significant part in maintaining liver health and preventing conditions such as non-alcoholic fatty liver disease, steatohepatitis and cholestatic liver disease. In obesity, the gut microbiome is altered, and gut-barrier function is compromised. Disruption of the mucosal barrier results in the release of microbial products that contribute to liver disease by inducing inflammation of the liver. Non-alcoholic fatty liver disease, a condition in which fat is deposited in the liver, is associated with obesity, metabolic syndrome and type 2 diabetes. It is also associated with increased gut permeability due to changes in the microbiome. This, along with the toxic metabolites released by non-beneficial microorganisms, likely plays a role in producing a chronic, low-grade inflammatory state that contributes to the development of obesity and its associated metabolic diseases. If left unchecked, non-alcoholic fatty liver disease can progress to non-alcoholic steatohepatitis, which can lead to liver cirrhosis through inflammation and scarring. Cirrhosis is an extreme end stage of chronic liver disease and is likely compounded by disturbed gut functioning.

3 The gut–skin axis

Our skin and the lining of the gut have some similarities in that they are epithelial tissues, which serve as barriers preventing unwanted organisms and substances entering our body. But their connections go beyond that. Conditions such as inflammatory bowel disease can sometimes be accompanied by skin lesions, and there is growing evidence that disturbed gut microbe populations and/or a leaky gut could contribute to skin conditions such as dermatitis, psoriasis and acne.

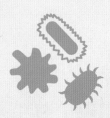

The gut and immune health

We know that a healthy gut microbiome helps ferment dietary fibres, leading to the production of beneficial substances, including some that promote a robust immune system. Certain components of the human microbiome, such as lipopolysaccharides from bacterial cell walls, can trigger inflammatory responses, whereas some microbial products have anti-inflammatory responses.

Impaired gut-barrier function is associated with an immune response triggered by opportunistic pathogens, which act directly on the epithelial cells, or penetrate the intestinal mucosa. This, in turn, activates the release of inflammatory cytokines, leading to inflammation in affected tissues. In a vicious circle, these cytokines also further disrupt gut-barrier function, leading to greater intestinal permeability.

The gut and pancreatic health

The pancreas is a major organ that is fundamental to metabolic health. It has two major functions: it produces key enzymes for the digestive system, including peptidases to break down proteins, lipases to digest fats and amylases for carbohydrates, and it also produces hormones such as insulin and glucagon. Increased gut permeability can disrupt the normal functioning of the pancreas. There is evidence that this happens when bacteria leak from the gut to the pancreas, causing inflammation in the tissues of the pancreas. Excessive alcohol intake can also increase gut permeability and may trigger inflammation of the pancreas.

Type 2 diabetes

Type 2 diabetes is a metabolic disorder that is characterised by high blood glucose and insulin resistance. It also appears to be associated with increased intestinal permeability. Accumulating evidence indicates that there are quantitative and qualitative differences in the gut microbiome of people with type 2 diabetes compared to individuals without type 2 diabetes.

Type 1 diabetes

Type 1 diabetes is an autoimmune disorder in which there is an absolute insulin deficiency due to the body's own T-cells destroying cells in the pancreas, known as the islets of Langerhans. Increased intestinal permeability has been reported in people with type 1 diabetes, and even precedes the clinical onset of the disease. This indicates the microbial environment and the integrity of the small intestine may play a role.

MAINTAINING GOOD GUT HEALTH CAN HELP PREVENT DISEASE

* A diet featuring a variety of healthy foods that contain adequate dietary fibre will help support your beneficial gut bacteria, as well as your digestive health and general wellbeing.

* Foods that are high in added sugar or highly processed are best avoided, as they may contribute to intestinal inflammation.

* Along with good nutrition, treatments that populate the microbiome with beneficial gut bacteria may help improve the functioning of the gut and alleviate inflammatory conditions related to poor gut health.

 Type 2 diabetes appears to be associated with increased intestinal permeability.

Leaky gut, inflammation and metabolic health

As we have seen, there is emerging evidence to suggest that a 'leaky' gut (increased intestinal permeability) is associated with a variety of disorders such as intestinal and liver diseases, obesity-related type 2 diabetes, and autoimmune disorders including type 1 diabetes. A leaky gut may contribute to systemic malfunctioning, and it may even be a primary causative factor in the development of some diseases, and further exacerbate them.

The gut barrier consists of a single layer of epithelial cells, protected by a mucus layer. In a healthy gut, the epithelial cells that line the gut are connected by tight junction proteins. This physical and biochemical barrier is selectively permeable, allowing beneficial nutrients to pass through and be absorbed, but stopping potentially harmful substances and microorganisms from entering the body from the GI tract.

In essence, our gut is a first line of defence in our immune system – and 70–80 per cent of the body's immune cells are found in the gut.

We now know, however, that the gut barrier can be disrupted by a poor diet, especially one that is low in dietary fibre and contains a lot of poor-quality processed foods high in salt, added sugars and saturated fats. Such a diet leads to increased intestinal permeability, more commonly known as a leaky gut.

In a leaky gut, foreign materials and toxins that normally do not enter the body will 'leak' through the gaps in the epithelial cells, causing low-level inflammation in the affected tissues. This inflammation occurs when the body tries to neutralise or eliminate foreign materials by releasing chemical messengers that draw immune cells to the area to deal with the invaders.

These observations may also provide an insight into the low level of inflammation that is typically associated with obesity and metabolic disorders – that is, a leaky gut allows increased entry of inflammatory microbial components into the body. In response, the body releases pro-inflammatory mediators to combat the foreign substances, resulting in an immune response, and subsequently inflammation. This helps explain why a low degree of inflammation appears to be a common phenomenon in obesity and type 2 diabetes.

LEAKY GUT AND THE
VICIOUS CIRCLE OF INFLAMMATION

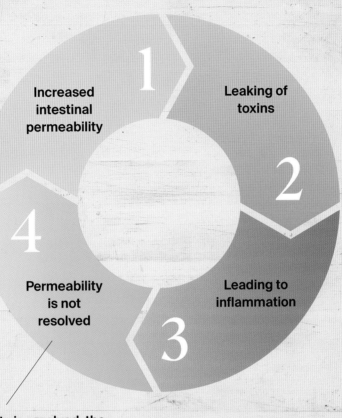

1 Increased intestinal permeability

2 Leaking of toxins

3 Leading to inflammation

4 Permeability is not resolved

If permeability is resolved, the gut is restored. Following the CSIRO Healthy Gut Diet, which includes beneficial nutrients for good gut health, can help.

 Our gut is a first line of defence in our immune system – and 70–80 per cent of the body's immune cells are found in the gut.

Gut health: key points

Eating plenty of fibre (see pages 22–27) and staying hydrated helps keep digested food moving efficiently and regularly.

Many functions of the GI tract, including muscular and secretory activities, are controlled by its own nervous system, called the enteric nervous system.

Your gut and your immune system are highly connected. Many of the cells of your immune system are located within the tissues of the gut.

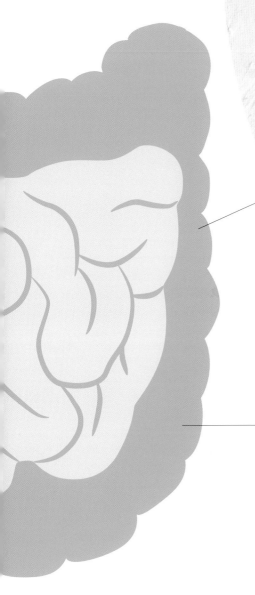

A normal gut barrier will not only keep your gut healthy but also the rest of the body healthy. To maintain a healthy gut barrier a balanced and diverse diet is critical.

Most gut microbes are present within the large bowel. If you want to influence them, food components and probiotics need to survive the upper GI tract. Prebiotic fibres (see page 52) are ideal.

The form of your stools is a useful indicator of digestive health (see page 215).

LIFESTYLE FACTORS THAT INFLUENCE GUT HEALTH

As well as diet, many lifestyle factors can influence the health of our gut. Some of these are described below.

Exercise

Exercise can assist with maintaining bowel movements. A sedentary lifestyle is associated with increased risk of poor health and disease, including colorectal cancer. A combination of overconsumption of food and a lack of exercise can lead to obesity, a condition associated with detrimental physiological changes, including a leaky gut (see page 42), and shifts in the gut microbe population's profile and activities.

Smoking

Smoking is a risk factor for colorectal cancer, as well as for cancers of the mouth, oesophagus, stomach, pancreas and liver. While there may be several mechanisms to explain this, particles in the air, including toxic particles from smoke, can reach the large bowel via the mucus clearance process of the lungs, and may negatively impact colorectal tissues. Fresh, unpolluted air is good for your gut.

Alcohol

Regular excessive consumption of alcohol can have adverse effects on our body, including the gut. Too much alcohol in one sitting can often lead to diarrhoea and gastrointestinal discomfort. If you consume alcohol, ensure it is only in moderate quantities. Alcohol is also a risk factor for colerectal, pancreatic and liver cancers.

Stress

The gut and the brain interact. Messages via our nervous and endocrine systems are sent in both directions. Anxiety and stress can influence bowel function and are linked to increased risk of irritable bowel syndrome. Finding ways to de-stress will benefit your gut.

Sleeping and eating patterns

Many of our body's activities have daily rhythms that have adjusted to factors, such as when we eat and when we sleep, in our day/night cycle. When we travel to different time zones, or we suddenly move to overnight shift work, our eating and sleeping times can also shift. Our body, including our gut, takes time to adjust. This disruption to our circadian rhythms can negatively impact gut health, especially if it occurs regularly. Maintaining a stable eating and sleeping routine will help your gut to digest food and provide stool regularity.

Travel, sanitation and infections

Travel, especially to some overseas areas, heightens the risk of contracting and spreading infectious agents, such as bacteria and viruses, including those causing diarrhoea. Some infections may lead to long-term gastrointestinal problems, including irritable bowel syndrome. When travelling, we may be exposed to different bacteria and viruses than those we are exposed to in our usual everyday environments, but there is also a greater risk due to poorer sanitisation practices in some countries. Travel can also bring people together in ways that allow infectious agents to spread. Plan ahead and know your hygiene needs when you travel. Always maintain robust personal hygiene practices, and be aware of where all your food and water has come from, and how it has been handled, cooked or stored.

THE INFLUENCE OF DIETARY COMPONENTS OTHER THAN FIBRE

Consuming foods from all food groups is important for overall health. For gut health, the many types of dietary fibre play particularly important roles. However, there are many other elements in our food which, when consumed in appropriate amounts, can contribute to optimal gut function. There are also foods we may wish to avoid or minimise in our diet to support our gut health.

The reason dietary fibre has such a profound influence on our gut is that it consists of many substances that are not digested in the upper gut and are therefore able to reach the large intestine, where the majority of our gut microbes reside. Other dietary components, as described below, are more readily digested, but may still have some effect on the gut.

Dietary protein

Proteins are important building blocks for the cells of our body, including muscle, and also our gut tissues. Most protein is digested in the small intestine, but some can reach the large intestine, where it can also be used by the resident microbes for growth and metabolism. Consuming a diet high in some protein sources (e.g. processed meats), but also lacking in dietary fibre, can lead to the production of potentially toxic by-products of fermentation within the large intestine, such as ammonia. While such a diet may not have any health impacts in the short term, it may result in poor gut health and more serious health problems if maintained over the long term.

Dietary fats

Although dietary fats and oils may sometimes be regarded negatively, especially as an excess of fat in Western-style diets is associated with obesity and poor health outcomes, our body requires healthy unsaturated fats (such as avocado, nuts and seeds) for its normal functioning. Some dietary fats can reach the large intestine, but their impact on the gut and gut microbes is relatively poorly researched. However, some experimental evidence suggests that healthy oils, such as the omega 3 oils found in oily fish, might benefit tissues of the gut.

Dietary phenolic compounds

Plant foods, such as wholegrains, fruits, vegetables, legumes, nuts and seeds, are rich sources of phenolic compounds, which have an antioxidant capacity. In addition to providing flavour, aroma and colour, these compounds have an important role in health, as they help protect our tissues from damage caused by free radical oxygen molecules in our food and in our environment. There is also good evidence that many phenolic compounds may benefit the gut by reducing populations of potentially harmful bacteria that may contribute to disease.

MEAT SUBSTITUTES

There has been a rapid and recent development of plant protein being released into the market, especially for sausages and patties. Typically, soy or pea protein is used, although other sources may become more popular in the future. Soy protein is widely consumed throughout the world and is generally regarded as safe. Nevertheless, whether using soy as the major source of protein is beneficial or detrimental to gut health deserves further research.

PROBIOTICS, PREBIOTICS AND POSTBIOTICS

Many of us have heard of – and use – probiotics. There is some evidence that the use of probiotics has beneficial effects on gut health by improving the balance of microbes, as well as immune and gut-barrier functions.

Probiotics

A probiotic is a live microbe consumed to bring about a health benefit. Probiotics are now one of the most widely recognised means by which people seek to improve their gut health, and the number of probiotic products on the market continues to grow. As indicated in our previous book, the effectiveness of each of these products is not always clear, and we encourage people to seek information from companies about whether their particular probiotic formulation has been thoroughly tested and shown to provide gut health benefits, or any other effects that are claimed or implied.

Prebiotics

Similarly, there is an increased awareness of prebiotics. A prebiotic is a dietary component, such as certain dietary fibres, which stimulates the growth of microbes that lead to health benefits. Many people may be eating foods – such as vegetables and fruits, and even breads – that contain prebiotic dietary fibres, without realising it. Many foods contain the prebiotic inulin, a polysaccharide found in many fruits and vegetables, which is added to a variety of products including some yoghurts.

Synbiotic

A synbiotic is a probiotic in combination with a prebiotic, with the intent of inducing synergistic effects. Ideally, the prebiotic is a substance used by the probiotic to facilitate its health benefits. Synbiotics can occur naturally during fermentation of foods, with some also now being formulated by manufacturers.

Multi-strain probiotics

Multi-strain probiotic products contain more than one type of probiotic. As each type of microbe has its own characteristics, and potentially produces a distinct range of substances, or has narrowly defined health benefits, combinations of probiotics could provide greater benefits than consuming one type of probiotic. The human gut contains hundreds of different types of microbes all working together, so supplements with combinations of probiotics may become more prevalent in the future.

Postbiotics

A relatively new category, postbiotics include substances produced by microbes (including probiotics) which, when consumed or administered in some way, may lead to a health benefit. Each of the many hundreds of different types of microbes in the human gut has the potential to produce many different types of substances that can influence physiology and benefit health. However, scientists are still a long way off identifying the majority of these substances and gaining a good understanding of what they all do. Nevertheless, the benefits of some of these compounds are known, and more products in this category are likely to be developed in the coming years.

There is some evidence that the use of probiotics may have beneficial effects on gut disorders.

THE POTENTIAL BENEFITS OF PROBIOTICS AND PREBIOTICS

The use of probiotics and prebiotics is usually associated with improvements in gut health. However, benefits may extend beyond the gut, with growing evidence suggesting that our gut microbes influence many, if not most, bodily systems.

A healthy population of gut microbes:

* is known to play an important part in maintaining an effective immune system, and may help to minimise some infections and inflammation

* may influence our brain, including our mood and levels of anxiety

* may help maintain the health of our skin

* assists in optimal metabolic functioning.

We should consume a diet containing foods that will feed and maintain a healthy population of gut microbes. Many plant-based foods contain fibres that act as prebiotics. A healthy diet with sufficient quantities of these foods will help maintain a healthy population of gut microbes.

 Many plant-based foods contain fibres that act as prebiotics.

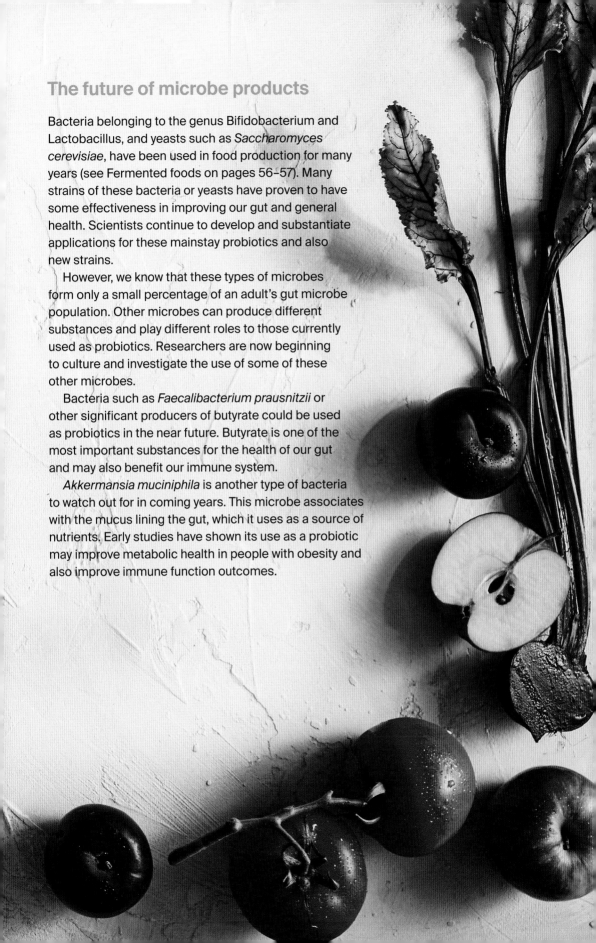

The future of microbe products

Bacteria belonging to the genus Bifidobacterium and Lactobacillus, and yeasts such as *Saccharomyces cerevisiae*, have been used in food production for many years (see Fermented foods on pages 56–57). Many strains of these bacteria or yeasts have proven to have some effectiveness in improving our gut and general health. Scientists continue to develop and substantiate applications for these mainstay probiotics and also new strains.

However, we know that these types of microbes form only a small percentage of an adult's gut microbe population. Other microbes can produce different substances and play different roles to those currently used as probiotics. Researchers are now beginning to culture and investigate the use of some of these other microbes.

Bacteria such as *Faecalibacterium prausnitzii* or other significant producers of butyrate could be used as probiotics in the near future. Butyrate is one of the most important substances for the health of our gut and may also benefit our immune system.

Akkermansia muciniphila is another type of bacteria to watch out for in coming years. This microbe associates with the mucus lining the gut, which it uses as a source of nutrients. Early studies have shown its use as a probiotic may improve metabolic health in people with obesity and also improve immune function outcomes.

FERMENTED FOODS

Fermentation is the process by which microbes, such as yeasts and bacteria, break down organic materials and convert simple carbohydrates and sugars into alcohols and acids, under conditions with little or no oxygen.

Humans have used fermentation for millennia, commonly for production of alcoholic drinks from a wide range of fruits, vegetables and grains, and even milk. Fermentation is also used for the preservation of foods, through the ability of the acids produced by fermentation to inhibit the growth of microbes that can cause spoilage and illness.

The acid substances and other fermentation by-products also add complexity to the taste of the food, creating new and interesting flavours in dishes.

The resurgence in interest in fermented foods is driven by a perception that they are intrinsically beneficial. The jury is still out regarding the type of health benefits of these foods, but fermentation can create unique flavours for vegetables, which are low in kilojoules and high in fibre – so why not give them a go? Popular fermented foods include:

* kimchi
* sauerkraut
* yoghurt
* cheese
* kombucha
* natto.

Here are some of the ways they may be of benefit:

* Many of the bacteria or yeasts found in fermented products are the same or similar to those which have been used as probiotics.

* The fermentation process releases beneficial compounds not readily accessible in non-fermented products – or the microbes themselves may generate additional beneficial substances that were not present in the original food.

* Fermentation may make some components easier to digest. Lactose, a sugar that some people find hard to digest, can be converted into other less problematic sugars in fermented yoghurt and various fermented milk drinks.

* Fermented vegetables are often rich in fibre, vitamins and minerals, which can benefit health.

If you have considered fermenting, but are not sure where to start, try the recipes on the following pages, which are free of added salt and sugar. (Commercial products may be high in salt.)

Rainbow vegetable pickles

2 cups sliced vegetables,
such as cucumber, asparagus,
carrot, radish, cauliflower florets,
zucchini and artichoke

Pickling liquid

1½ cups (375 ml) white vinegar

2 teaspoons mustard seeds

2 teaspoons celery seeds

Spiced salt-free
sauerkraut
PAGE 62

1. Wash two 500 ml jars in hot soapy water, then rinse and dry well. Pack in the sliced vegetables.
2. Combine the vinegar, mustard seeds, celery seeds and 1½ cups (375 ml) water in a saucepan and bring to a simmer over high heat. Pour the hot pickling liquid into the jars. You should have enough to completely cover the vegetables; if not, make up a little more of the liquid to make sure they are fully submerged.

3. Leave to cool on the bench, then transfer to the fridge to cool completely. You can eat the pickles immediately, or store them in the fridge for up to 2 months. When pickling foods, it is important to have a good seal in the jar for optimal fermentation and to prevent excess growth of pathogens, so before storing, check your jars are sealed tight.

1 cup = 1 unit Vegetables ✻ **4 g fibre**

WAYS TO ENJOY PICKLED VEGETABLES

✻ Toss 2 tablespoons through your salads for extra tang and crunch.
✻ Serve as a condiment with steak and pork to help cut through the richness of the meat.
✻ Roughly chop and add to avocado toast in the morning.
✻ Serve alongside eggs.

Homemade kimchi
PAGE 60

MAKES: 2 X
1 LITRE JARS

PREP: 1 HR 20 MINS, PLUS
FERMENTING TIME

Homemade kimchi

5 garlic cloves, roughly chopped

4 cm piece ginger, peeled and roughly chopped

2–4 tablespoons dried chilli flakes (depending on how much heat you like)

1 small onion, roughly chopped

3 tablespoons dulse or finely ground kelp (optional)

½ cup (125 ml) no-added-sugar kombucha

1.3 kg Chinese cabbage (wombok) or savoy cabbage

1 apple, thinly sliced into matchsticks

1 carrot, thinly sliced into matchsticks

12 spring onions, trimmed and thinly sliced

1. Prepare a chilli paste by blitzing the garlic, ginger, chilli flakes, onion, dulse or kelp (if using) and kombucha in a food processor until combined.

2. Remove the bottom core from the cabbage (about 4 cm) and set aside for later (you'll use it to weigh down the kimchi). Roughly chop the cabbage and place in a large bowl. Add the apple, carrot and spring onion and toss together well.

3. Take a big handful (about 1½ cups) of the cabbage mixture and place in a blender. Add 3 tablespoons water and blitz to liquidise the vegetables into a sort of brine. Add another 2–3 tablespoons water if needed. Pour the brine and the chilli paste over the cabbage mixture in the bowl.

4. Mix everything together really well with your hands (wear prep gloves to avoid burning from the chilli) or a pair of tongs, scrunching and massaging as you go to help soften the veggies and release their liquid. Cover with a tea towel and leave on the bench for 1 hour, scrunching regularly, until the leaves have softened.

5. Scoop the kimchi into clean jars (see tip), packing it down as you go with your fingers or the back of a fork. Stop when the jars are three-quarters full and top up with enough water to completely cover the cabbage. Halve the reserved cabbage core and add to the jars, pushing down the cabbage and allowing the liquid to spill over. Lightly screw on the lid, keeping it a little loose. Place the jars in a cool spot away from direct sunlight and leave to ferment for 3–5 days. During this time you will start to see bubbles and the flavour will become pleasantly sour.

6. Every day you'll need to 'burp' the kimchi to remove excess pressure. To do this, unscrew the lid, and push down any of the contents that have risen above the liquid.

7. On day four or five, taste the kimchi and if it's ready, move it to the fridge, where it will keep for up to 12 months.

1 cup = 1 unit Vegetables ✳ **6 g fibre**

TIPS

✳ Wash the jars in hot soapy water to ensure they're clean before packing in the kimchi.

✳ Dulse is a red edible seaweed. We use it here to provide an umami flavour enhancer in the absence of the more traditional salt and soy sauce.

✳ The kombucha kick-starts the fermentation process, feeding the vegetables with good microbes, which encourages these good microbes to reproduce at a faster rate, crowding out the bad microbes. If you can't find no-added-sugar kombucha, just create more of the brine by doubling the quantities. You'll need to ferment the kimchi for a bit longer, about 6–7 days.

✳ Ensure the cabbage is always pushed below the liquid! This is THE most important part of the fermentation process. If your cabbage core doesn't keep it submerged, place half an apple on top, then use the lid to press everything down and screw the lid on so nothing can rise up.

Spiced salt-free
sauerkraut
PAGE 62

Homemade
Kimchi

MAKES: 2 X
1 LITRE JARS

PREP: 30 MINS, PLUS
FERMENTING TIME

Spiced salt-free sauerkraut

1.3 kg green cabbage

1 tablespoon caraway seeds

1 tablespoon coriander seeds

2 teaspoons fennel seeds

1 tablespoon crushed black peppercorns

½ cup (125 ml) no-added sugar kombucha

1. Peel off the two outer leaves of the cabbage, then remove the bottom core (about 4 cm) and set aside for later (you will use these to weigh down the sauerkraut). Finely shred the remaining cabbage, either with a sharp chef's knife or by pushing it through the grater attachment of a food processor. Place the cabbage in a large bowl.

2. Take a big handful (about 1½ cups) of the cabbage and place in a blender. Add 3 tablespoons water and blitz to liquidise into a sort of cabbage brine. Add another 2–3 tablespoons water if needed. Pour the brine over the cabbage.

3. Finely grind the whole spices using a mortar and pestle or spice grinder. Scatter over the cabbage and massage in with your hands, scrunching as you go to help soften the cabbage and release its liquid. This raw cabbage juice is rich in lactic acid, which will help with the fermentation process. Allow to sit for 20 minutes, then scrunch and massage again. Pour in the kombucha and toss to combine.

WAYS TO ENJOY SAUERKRAUT

* Add to baked potatoes or salads.
* Serve as a condiment with fish or red meat.
* Use in sandwiches, wraps and tacos for extra flavour.

4. Tightly pack the cabbage into clean glass jars (see tip) and pour over any liquid left behind in the bowl. You want the cabbage to be entirely covered by liquid, so add water to top up the jars as needed. Halve the reserved cabbage core and tear the reserved cabbage leaves, and use to push down the cabbage until it is completely submerged in the liquid. The key to a successful ferment is to ensure the vegetables are in an 'anaerobic' condition (meaning without oxygen), so this step is essential for the process to work.

5. Lightly place the lids on the jars and put them on a baking tray (this will catch any seeping juices). Leave in a room-temperature spot away from direct sunlight, checking each day to see if the sauerkraut needs a top up of water, or if you need to push the cabbage back down under the liquid with the back of a fork. Every few days you'll need to 'burp' the sauerkraut to remove excess pressure. To do this, unscrew the lid and push down any of the contents that have risen above the liquid.

6. Continue checking for 3–5 days. To tell if the sauerkraut is ready, you must use your senses: it will be bubbly and taste pleasantly sour; it should smell fermented without being offensive; and it should retain its fresh white and green colouring, without any sign of mould or black/grey spots. The timing will vary, depending on where you are; the process is faster in hot environments and takes a little longer in cool environments.

7. Once fermentation is complete, store in the fridge for up to 6 months.

1 cup = 1 unit Vegetables ✳ **6 g fibre**

TIPS

✳ Wash the jars in hot soapy water to ensure they're clean before packing in the cabbage.

✳ Ensure the cabbage is always pushed below the liquid! This is THE most important part of the fermentation process. If your cabbage core doesn't keep it submerged, place half an apple on top, then use the lid to press everything down and screw the lid on so nothing can rise up.

✳ The kombucha kick-starts the fermentation process, feeding the fermenting vegetables with good microbes, which encourages the good microbes to reproduce at a faster rate, crowding out the bad microbes. If you can't find no-added-sugar kombucha, just create more of the brine by doubling the quantities. You'll need to ferment the sauerkraut for a bit longer, about 6–7 days.

✳ Avoid heating your sauerkraut, as this will destroy the beneficial bacteria that you've carefully cultivated through the fermentation process.

✳ Sauerkraut is rich in beneficial bacteria. If you are new to sauerkraut, start slowly, with just a small forkful every few days to see how your gut responds before having it more regularly and in larger quantities.

PART TWO

THE CSIRO HEALTHY gut EATING PLAN

WHAT IS THE CSIRO HEALTHY GUT EATING PLAN?

Following the CSIRO Healthy Gut Eating Plan is about including foods rich in dietary fibre and resistant starch in your meals, in order to reach an adequate intake of dietary fibre, daily. To help you achieve this goal, in this section we introduce the core food groups, outline the daily food guide and suggest fibre staples and resistant starch options. We also share tips and meal ideas to help you to integrate good fibre choices into your everyday diet.

> * If you are looking for FODMAP-friendly suggestions, please refer to book 1, *The CSIRO Healthy Gut Diet*, or speak to an accredited practising dietitian or your healthcare team to help you adjust the CSIRO Healthy Gut Eating Plan to your needs.

Evidence shows that increasing the diversity and the total amount of fibre in your daily intake can improve the health of your gut at any age. Fibre diversity is reaching an adequate amount of dietary fibre through a variety of fibre-rich foods. Over time, maintaining a healthier, nutrient-dense diet that is rich in fibre can also help prevent or delay the onset of chronic diseases and some cancers, especially bowel cancer.

This eating plan isn't about weight loss; it's about using wholefoods wisely and in good portions, for good health. The eating plan is consistent with the core principles of the CSIRO's nutrition research, providing an eating pattern that is higher in protein, healthy fats and low-GI carbohydrates, choosing wholegrain, nutrient-dense ingredients with the emphasis on dietary fibre.

 This eating plan is about using wholefoods wisely and in good portions, for good health.

Introducing the core food groups

To help you incorporate a range of nutrients into your everyday diet, we have grouped foods into core food groups, according to the primary or key nutrients provided (see page 70). As a result of feedback we have received from readers of the first book, we have included the total amount of daily units required for a 7500 kJ standard healthy gut plan, suiting individuals who are more active. The 6500 kJ plan also remains and is suitable for those who are less active, as well as smaller individuals.

If you require more than 7500 kJ a day to maintain your weight, add 1 unit of wholegrain high-fibre breads, cereals and legumes, and 1 unit of lean meat, fish, poultry, eggs, tofu and legumes, increasing your intake to 8500 kJ. Remember, the indulgences are optional, and are not encouraged to increase your total energy intake.

Step 1

Look at the table of recommended daily units for each food group on the following page and make a selection based on what you feel most suits your lifestyle. For example, if you are an office worker with limited exercise, maybe the 6500 kJ plan is best suited for you. If you are a larger or a more active person, try the 7500 kJ plan.

Step 2

Once you have decided on the plan that you feel will fit your needs, your next step is to take action. To do this, look through the foods from each of the food groups in your daily food guide and highlight those that you like and those that you will try. Use the highlighted foods to make a shopping list, and start to build your gut-friendly pantry, fridge and freezer by including these foods.

Step 3

Now it's time to look through the recipes and begin building your meal plans. Refer to the units provided on the recipe pages to make up your daily unit requirements and the fibre flag to make sure you are reaching your dietary fibre targets. By using the units as described in the recommended units table, you can achieve a balanced dietary intake, including essential vitamins and minerals.

START OUT SLOWLY

If you are starting to add more fibre to your diet, it may be worth gradually increasing the fibre a little at a time, to help your gut adjust. For example, you could start by adding 1–2 tablespoons of legumes to a meal once a day for the first week, increasing to 3–4 tablespoons in the second week, and so on, until you are able to comfortably eat a full serve. Another way would be to eat half a high-fibre barley wrap each day for the first week, and a whole wrap each day for the second.

While your body and microbiome may take weeks to adjust, you will start to notice benefits straight away, with better bowel habits and a faster 'transit time', which means your body is moving food through your bowels faster; you may also start to recognise that you are feeling fuller for longer throughout the day. This is a good thing! By week two, your body should be settling into a rhythm with your higher-fibre diet and regular bowel movements. If you are experiencing discomfort or have not seen any improvements within four weeks, please check in with your healthcare team.

 You will start to notice healthier gut benefits straight away.

RECOMMENDED DAILY UNITS FOR EACH FOOD GROUP

FOOD GROUP	NUMBER OF DAILY UNITS		AVERAGE NUTRIENT CONTENT PER UNIT				COMMENTS
	6500 kJ plan	7500 kJ plan	Fibre	Protein	Carbs	Total fat	
Wholegrain high-fibre breads, cereals and legumes	3	4	5 g	3 g	15 g	<1 g	Avoid added sugar and refined products. Rich in folate, fibre, B group vitamins and carbs.
Lean meat, fish, poultry, eggs, tofu and legumes	3	3	<1 g	20 g	0 g	5 g	Aim to have 3 fish meals each week. High in protein, zinc, vitamin B12 and iron.
Fruit	2	2	3 g	2 g	15 g	0 g	Source of fibre, vitamin C, antioxidants and polyphenols.
Vegetables	5	5	3 g	3.5 g	4.5 g	1 g	Good source of magnesium, vitamins A, B6 and C, fibre, antioxidants and polyphenols.
Dairy	3	3	<1 g	9 g	9 g	4.5 g	Choose products with no added sugar. Rich in protein, calcium, B12 and zinc.
Healthy fats and oils	4	6	0 g	0 g	0 g	5 g	Source of vitamins A, E and K, antioxidants and omegas 3 and 6 fatty acids.
Indulgence foods	Limit to 9 units across the week		Low	Variable	Variable	Variable	Often high in salt, sugar and saturated fats, and energy dense. Choose sparingly .

YOUR DAILY FOOD GUIDE

In this part of the book, we share the foods that you need to include in your meals each day to get a balance of core nutrients. We have extended the range of foods from book one to give you more options.

All foods are grouped together based on the key nutrients they provide, with the weighted portions (e.g. grams and/or cups) giving you 1 unit, while still maintaining a similar energy and nutrient density per unit. That means, within each food group, you can swap your foods around. So, if you do not want ½ cup of cereal for breakfast, you can swap this for 1 slice of wholegrain bread OR ½ a wholemeal English muffin.

HEALTHY GUT PRINCIPLES

* Use low-GI, wholegrain food varieties that are rich in fibre and resistant starch (see pages 96–103 for resistant starch foods).

* Choose a mix of fibre-rich foods in your day to get a balance of insoluble and soluble fibre (as well as resistant starch).

* Try to include legumes in your meals at least twice a week. They are included in the lean meat, fish, poultry, eggs and tofu group, as well as the wholegrain breads and cereals group.

* Aim to meet your units of vegetables and fruit each and every day; leaving the skin on adds to your fibre intake.

Wholegrain, high-fibre breads, cereals and legumes

Breads

* 1 slice wholegrain, rye* or pumpernickel bread
* ½ wholegrain, rye* or pumpernickel bread roll
* ½ wholemeal, rye*, rice-based pita bread (e.g. Mountain Bread wrap)
* ½ wholemeal English muffin
* 2 slices wholegrain, rye* or seeded crispbread
  (e.g. Ryvita or 9 Grains Vita-Weat)
* 25 g wholegrain/wholemeal breadcrumbs

High soluble-fibre, low-GI cereal

* ⅓ cup high-fibre breakfast cereal flakes or no-added-sugar muesli — those
  containing mixed grains or wholegrains, such as buckwheat, puffed wheat
  or rice, are good sources of resistant starch
* ⅓ cup uncooked rolled oats* (⅔ cup cooked oats made with water)

Legumes

* 100 g cooked or tinned lentils, beans, chickpeas or other legumes
  (e.g. kidney beans*, adzuki beans*, black-eyed beans*, butter beans)

Low-GI, high-starch vegetables

* 150 g sweet potato*
* 150 g potato

Other grains

* 3 tablespoons pure maize corn flour*, potato starch*, chickpea flour*,
  green banana flour*, millet* or rice flour*
* 2 level tablespoons wholemeal plain or self-raising flour, arrowroot flour,
  buckwheat flour
* ¾ cup cooked millet, barley, freekeh, farro, quinoa*
* ½ cup cooked basmati rice*, buckwheat*, couscous, semolina, polenta
* ½ cup cooked wholemeal low-GI pasta
* 3 cups popcorn (⅙ cup dry kernels) — plain, unsalted, no added fat

Note: Foods with * next to them are higher in resistant starch.

FOOD GROUP	PORTIONS EQUAL TO 1 UNIT
Lean meat, fish, poultry, eggs, tofu and legumes	* 100 g (raw weight) lean lamb, beef, veal or kangaroo (500 g maximum a week) * 100 g (raw weight) fresh fish or seafood (minimum twice a week) * 100 g (raw weight) lean chicken, turkey, duck or pork * 2 x 50–55 g whole eggs (large) * 170 g tofu or Quorn products * 150 g tempeh * 100 g textured vegetable protein (TVP) * 150 g cooked or tinned lentils*, beans, chickpeas* or other legumes (e.g. kidney beans*, adzuki beans*, black-eyed beans*, butter beans)
Fruit	* 1 medium apple, 1 medium pear, 1 orange, 1 tangerine, 1 fresh fig, 1 peach, 1 small banana (slightly green banana*) * 2 small fruit (e.g. kiwifruit, apricots, plums, nectarines, feijoas) * 1 cup diced fresh, frozen or tinned fruit – no juice (e.g. berries, pineapple, mango, cherries, grapes)

Note: Foods with * next to them are higher in resistant starch.

FOOD GROUP	PORTIONS EQUAL TO 1 UNIT
Vegetables	* 1 cup cooked or frozen vegetables (e.g. broccoli, cauliflower, carrot, green beans, green peas*) * 2 cups raw leafy green vegetables (e.g. lettuce, spinach, watercress) or raw salad vegetables (e.g. tomato, cucumber, radish, fennel) and herbs * 1 cup cooked broad beans or edamame * 1 cup fermented vegetables (e.g. kimchi) * 5 pieces of sundried tomato (use sparingly) **You can enjoy unlimited vegetables on the Healthy Gut Eating Plan:** (e.g. artichoke*, asparagus, bamboo shoots, beetroot, bok choy, broccoli, brussels sprouts, cabbage, capsicum, carrot, cauliflower, celeriac, celery, choy sum, choko, cucumber, eggplant, endive, fennel, green beans, green peas, kale, kohlrabi, leek, lettuce, mushrooms, okra, onion, parsnip, pumpkin, radicchio, radish, shallots, silverbeet, snow peas, spinach, spring onion, squash, tomato, turnip, zucchini)
Dairy	* 1 cup fresh or UHT plain, unflavoured regular milk, or calcium-enriched unsweetened soy, rice or almond milk (for non-dairy milk, aim for 100 mg calcium per 100 ml, depending on your individual needs) * 1 cup buttermilk * 20 g skim milk powder * ¾ cup plain, unflavoured reduced-fat yoghurt (Greek style), or low-fat, lactose-free soy yoghurt * ½ cup reduced-fat ricotta cheese * ½ cup cottage cheese * 40 g cheese (e.g. parmesan, Swiss, feta, mozzarella, bocconcini) * 40 g reduced-fat cream cheese

Note: Foods with * next to them are higher in resistant starch.

FOOD GROUP	PORTIONS EQUAL TO 1 UNIT
Healthy fats and oils	✳ 1 teaspoon oil (e.g. extra virgin olive oil, grapeseed oil, flaxseed oil (linseed oil), sunflower oil, macadamia oil)
	✳ 1 teaspoon tahini (sesame butter), almond or other nut butters, oil-based pesto, curry paste
	✳ 1 tablespoon avocado
	✳ 1 tablespoon hummus*
	✳ 1 teaspoon Nuttelex
	✳ 1 teaspoon olive oil or canola margarine
	✳ 2 teaspoons unsalted nuts or seeds (e.g. cashews*, almonds, pecans, macadamias, walnuts, Brazil nuts, pistachios, pine nuts, pumpkin seeds/pepitas, poppy seeds, sesame seeds, flaxseeds/linseeds)
	✳ 3 teaspoons chia seeds
	✳ 2 teaspoons almond meal
	✳ 1 teaspoon coconut flakes/desiccated coconut
	✳ 20 g olives
	✳ 2 teaspoons whole-egg mayonnaise
	✳ 2 teaspoons sour cream or crème fraîche

Note: Foods with * next to them are higher in resistant starch.

FOOD GROUP	PORTIONS EQUAL TO 1 UNIT
Indulgence foods Indulgence foods are optional and not encouraged to be part of your everyday intake.	✳ 150 ml wine ✳ 30 ml spirits ✳ 375 ml beer ✳ 20 g chocolate ✳ 45 g sweet spreads (e.g. jam, honey, marmalade or maple syrup) ✳ 30 g sweet lollies ✳ 20 g potato chips, corn chips or savoury snack foods ✳ 8 hot chips ✳ 40 g tomato sauce or chutney ✳ 1 small muesli bar ✳ 2 small plain sweet biscuits ✳ 40 g slice of cake or sweet bun ✳ 10–12 rice crackers

Note: Foods with * next to them are higher in resistant starch.

'EAT FREELY' ITEMS

In addition to the daily food guide on the previous pages, you can enjoy the following low-kilojoule beverages, herbs, spices and condiments freely throughout the day, to boost your fibre intake and add variety and flavour.

Beverages

* black coffee
* black tea
* herbal tea
* unflavoured mineral or soda water

FRESH FLAVOUR BOOSTS

* **Infuse mineral or soda water with fruit and herbs:**
  - cucumber + mint
  - orange slices + rosemary sprigs
  - ginger + berries
  - strawberry + cucumber + mint
  - grapefruit + pomegranate
  - freshly squeezed lemon or lime juice and zest
  - sliced lemon + ginger

* **Steep herbs to make your own tea.** Add a handful of mint or lemon verbena leaves to boiling water.

* **Flavour black coffee with a dash of vanilla extract.** Or add a cinnamon stick or ground cacao nibs to infuse as it brews.

Herbs

All fresh and dried
herbs, including:

* basil
* bay leaves
* chives

* coriander
* dill
* marjoram
* mint
* oregano

* parsley
* rosemary
* sage
* tarragon
* thyme

COOKING WITH HERBS

* Dried herbs and woodier fresh herbs, such as rosemary, are typically added early in the cooking process, whereas delicate herbs, such as basil and coriander, are typically added towards the end of cooking or used as a garnish.

* **Herbs in world cuisines:**
  - Asian: coriander, mint, Thai basil, Vietnamese mint
  - French: tarragon, thyme, sage, rosemary
  - Italian: basil, oregano, parsley
  - Middle Eastern: parsley, mint, thyme
  - South American: coriander, thyme, oregano.

* **Favourite herb pairings for protein:**
  - seafood: dill, chives, tarragon, chervil
  - chicken: tarragon, coriander, marjoram, thyme
  - lamb: mint, oregano, thyme, rosemary
  - beef: thyme, rosemary, bay leaves
  - pork: rosemary, sage, thyme
  - turkey: sage, thyme, rosemary
  - legumes: most herbs, depending on the cuisine.

GET CREATIVE: SIMPLE SAUCES

Chimichurri: flat-leaf parsley + oregano + garlic + red wine vinegar + olive oil + chilli + coriander (optional).
Pair with: chargrilled meat, roast cauliflower steaks, chargrilled veg.

Pico de gallo: coriander + onion + lime juice + tomato + jalapeno (optional).
Pair with: burrito bowls, tacos.

Salsa verde: flat-leaf parsley + basil + red wine vinegar + capers + anchovies + garlic + lemon zest + olive oil.
Pair with: red meat, roasted veg.

Yoghurt herb sauce: natural yoghurt + garlic + lime or lemon juice + mint + dill.
Pair with: Mediterranean and Middle Eastern dishes.

Spices

Whole and ground spices, including:

* allspice
* cardamom
* chilli
* Chinese five-spice
* cinnamon
* cloves
* coriander (ground)
* cumin
* curry powder
* fennel seeds
* garam masala
* ginger
* mustard
* nutmeg
* paprika
* peppercorns
* star anise
* sumac
* turmeric.

COOKING WITH SPICES

* Most spices need to be added early in the cooking process to release their flavour and combine with the other ingredients in the dish. Spices are typically used in saucier dishes, such as curries and tagines, and in grain-based meals cooked using the absorption method, including risottos and pilafs, as well as in baked goods and as a rub for roasted meats and vegetables. While not technically spices, garlic and ginger are treated as spices in a culinary sense.

* **Spices in world cusines:**
    - Indian: cumin, ground coriander, garam masala, cardamom, turmeric
    - Mexican: paprika, garlic, cumin, chilli
    - Moroccan: cinnamon, paprika, cumin, turmeric
    - Thai: chilli, ground coriander, cardamom, cassia
    - Turkish: paprika, cinnamon, turmeric.

* **Favourite spice pairings for protein:**
    - seafood: ginger, garlic, white pepper, chilli, paprika
    - chicken: Chinese five-spice, paprika, allspice, cinnamon, nutmeg
    - lamb: fennel seeds, sumac, cumin, chilli
    - beef: mustard, paprika, pepper, cumin
    - chickpeas: paprika, cinnamon, cayenne pepper
    - lentils: cumin, turmeric, garam masala.

Sauces, pastes, powders, citrus, vinegar and seasonings

* cocoa powder
* fish sauce
* hoisin sauce
* horseradish
* kecap manis
* lemon juice
* lime juice
* mirin
* mustards (dijon, wholegrain)

* oyster sauce
* sambal oelek (chilli paste)
* soy sauce (salt reduced)
* sriracha chilli sauce
* stock cubes
* tomato passata
* vanilla extract

* verjuice
* vinegar (balsamic, red wine, rice wine, white wine)
* wasabi
* Worcestershire sauce.

COOKING WITH CONDIMENTS

* Condiments can be used to add additional flavour and moisture to just about anything – sandwiches, salad dressings, dipping sauces, marinades, fried rice, stir-fries, roasting glazes and other toppings.

* Choose products that contain as few ingredients as possible, and contain no or minimal added sugars, sweeteners and sodium. Fresher is better. If the product has a relatively short shelf life and requires refrigeration after opening, it is more likely to have fewer added ingredients. The exception is vinegar, which will keep at room temperature for a long time.

GET CREATIVE: EASY MARINADES

Try these flavour combinations with the below protein suggestions. Simply mix the ingredients together with the raw protein and leave in the fridge for 20 minutes before cooking.

- Tofu marinade: soy sauce + rice wine + ginger + sesame oil
- Tempeh marinade: sambal oelek + kecap manis + ginger
- Beef marinade: soy sauce + ginger + mirin + rice wine
- Stir-fry sauce: oyster sauce + soy sauce + sambal oelek + sesame oil.

FIBRE STAPLES

Set yourself up with a variety of high-fibre pantry and freezer staples that you can grab on the go or prepare into a quick meal. Keeping these items on hand will make it easier to follow a high-fibre diet.

Convenience foods are often highly processed and can be high in added sugar, salt, or saturated fat. To help you avoid reaching for these types of low-fibre foods, stock up on more of the following options.

IN THE PANTRY

* **Legumes,** such as dried or tinned, salt-reduced kidney beans, lentils, chickpeas, butter beans and four-bean mix, to add to salads, soups, curries and stir-fries.

* **Nuts and seeds,** such as cashews, chia seeds, almonds and pumpkin seeds/pepitas, to add to snacks such as yoghurt and fruit salad, and to salads and stir-fries.

* **High-fibre grains,** such as oats, pearl barley, wholegrain pasta and rice, wholemeal couscous and burghul — these staples are versatile and can be used as a base for many meals.

* **Wholegrain breads and high-fibre wraps**.

Wholegrain pasta

Wholegrain breads

Almonds

Oats

Beans, lentils, chickpeas and other legumes

Cashews

Chia seeds

87

IN THE FRIDGE

* **Fresh fruit and veggies** – buy only what you know you can eat to avoid spoilage. Storing produce properly, such as keeping fruit and vegetables in the crisper, will prolong their fridge life.

* **Yoghurt and dairy, or dairy-alternative milks and cheeses**, are good for gut health and bone health, and go perfectly with high-fibre foods such as wholegrain breads and cereals.

* **Tofu** – use in stir-fries, burgers and wraps.

IN THE FREEZER

* **Frozen peas, broad beans, edamame and other veggies** – add to pasta, curries, casseroles and slow-cooker meals.

* **Wholegrain bread** – try rye, sourdough and wholemeal. The denser, the better!

Fresh fruit and veg

Tofu

Yoghurt, milk and cheese

Frozen peas, broad beans and edamame

GOOD FIBRE CHOICES

It is important to eat a variety of foods from each food group. Some food groups are naturally higher in fibre than other food groups. For example, plant-based foods, such as grains and vegetables, are more fibrous than meat and dairy foods.

To help guide your choices, we've compiled a list of foods, arranged by group, with the food with the highest quantity of fibre given in each. An excellent source of fibre contains at least 7 grams of fibre per serve, and a good source of fibre contains at least 4 grams per serve.
   Use this as a tool to help you choose high-fibre foods when planning your own meals and snacks for home and at work, or for family members.

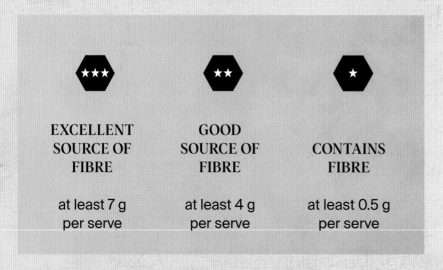

EXCELLENT SOURCE OF FIBRE	GOOD SOURCE OF FIBRE	CONTAINS FIBRE
at least 7 g per serve	at least 4 g per serve	at least 0.5 g per serve

 Plant-based foods, such as grains and vegetables, are more fibrous than meat and dairy foods.

Wholegrain breads and cereals	SERVING SIZE	FIBRE PER SERVE
★★★ **EXCELLENT FIBRE RATING** Wheat bran	30 g	12.5 g
★★ **GOOD FIBRE RATING** BARLEYmax™ cereals	30 g	6.0 g
Rolled oats (raw)	30 g	4.5 g
Oat bran	30 g	4.7 g
Mixed grain and rye crispbread e.g. Ryvita	2 crispbreads	4.0 g
Wholemeal pasta	75 g (cooked)	4.3 g
Rye grains	40 g (uncooked)	6.9 g
Barley grains (whole)	40 g	5.2 g
Quinoa	40 g (uncooked)	4.2 g
Wheat germ	30 g	6.0 g
Chickpea flour	20 g	4.2 g
★ **CONTAINS FIBRE** Wholewheat cereal biscuits e.g. Weet-Bix	30 g	2.8 g
Pumpernickel bread	1 thick slice	3.5 g
Wholemeal bread with seeds	1 slice	3.4 g
Rye bread	1 slice	2.3 g
Air-popped popcorn (no salt or fat)	3 cups	3.6 g
Sweet potato	150 g	3.9 g
Wild rice	40 g (uncooked)	2.5 g
Brown rice	40 g (uncooked)	1.4 g
Wholemeal wheat flour	20 g	2.2 g
Green banana starch	20 g	2.4 g

Lean meat, fish, poultry, eggs and tofu	SERVING SIZE	FIBRE PER SERVE
★★★ **EXCELLENT FIBRE RATING** Tempeh	150 g	9.8 g
★★ **GOOD FIBRE RATING** Tofu	170 g	6.0 g

Legumes		SERVING SIZE	FIBRE PER SERVE
★★★ **EXCELLENT FIBRE RATING**	Black beans	100 g	8.8 g
★★ **GOOD FIBRE RATING**	Cannellini beans	100 g	6.4 g
	Red kidney beans	100 g	6.5 g
	Chickpeas	100 g	5.7 g
	Brown lentils	100 g	5.2 g

Dairy		SERVING SIZE	FIBRE PER SERVE
★ **CONTAINS FIBRE**	Soy milk	1 cup	1.8 g
	Almond milk	1 cup	0.7 g

Fruit		SERVING SIZE	FIBRE PER SERVE
★★★ **EXCELLENT FIBRE RATING**	Passionfruit flesh	8 fruits (150 g)	20.0 g
	Pomegranate seeds	150 g	9.6 g
	Blackberries	150 g	9.2 g
	Raspberries	150 g	8.4 g
★★ **GOOD FIBRE RATING**	Blueberries	150 g	5.3 g
	Pink Lady apple	1 fruit	4.9 g
	Kiwifruit	2 fruits	4.7 g

Vegetables		SERVING SIZE	FIBRE PER SERVE
★★★ **EXCELLENT FIBRE RATING**	Boiled artichoke	1 cup	16.9 g
	Broad beans	1 cup	13.0 g
	Green peas	1 cup	9.8 g
	Celeriac	150 g	7.6 g
★★ **GOOD FIBRE RATING**	Corn on the cob	1 cup	6.7 g
	Carrots	150 g	5.1 g
	Beetroot (raw)	1 cup	5.1 g
	Parsnip	1 cup	4.5 g
	Brussels sprouts	1 cup	4.2 g
★ **CONTAINS FIBRE**	Raw spinach	150 g	3.8 g
	Broccoli	1 cup	3.4 g
	Red cabbage	1 cup	3.2 g
	Asparagus	1 cup	3.1 g
	Eggplant	1 cup	2.1 g
	Cauliflower	1 cup	1.4 g

Healthy fats and oils

		SERVING SIZE	FIBRE PER SERVE
★ CONTAINS FIBRE	Chia seeds	10 g	3.4 g
	Almonds, skin on	7 g	1 g
	Sunflower seeds	7 g	0.8 g
	Hazelnuts	7 g	0.7 g
	Pistachios	7 g	0.6 g
	Cashews, walnuts, Brazil nuts (skin on), pecans, macadamias	7 g	0.5 g
	Olives	20 g	0.5 g

Indulgences

		SERVING SIZE	FIBRE PER SERVE
★★★ EXCELLENT FIBRE RATING	Muesli bar with added fibre	1 bar	8.5 g
★ CONTAINS FIBRE	Wholemeal shortcrust pastry	25 g	2.6 g
	Wholemeal digestive biscuits	1.5 biscuits	1.5 g
	Fruit bun	40 g	1.4 g

Sunflower seeds

Olives

Hazelnuts

Pistachios

Chia seeds

95

RESISTANT STARCH FOODS

Here are some commonly consumed foods that are high in resistant starch. We also share some tips on how to add them into your everyday diet without too much fuss.

Under-ripe bananas and green banana starch

Under-ripe bananas are higher in resistant starch. The trick is to choose bananas that are on the greener side and eat them while they are still firm and before they become yellow, and before brown spots develop.

Slightly green bananas are safe to eat, although you may wish to avoid entirely green ones due to their slightly bitter taste and texture. Some people might also find that the high fibre content affects their digestion. If this is the case for you, revisit the section on introducing fibre to your diet on page 31.

Bananas make a great mid-morning snack, and travel well while they are still green, so they can be packed in a bag for work or school. You can also add bananas and banana starch to your breakfast cereal or porridge, a smoothie, a yoghurt and fruit and nut mix, or use in baked items such as muffins and bread, or a sweetened rice-based dessert.

As a general rule, fruits pair well with dairy foods (like milk and yoghurt), as well as plain grains (like rice and oats).

 Bananas make a great mid-morning snack, and travel well while they are still green.

BREAKFAST IN FIVE

* **Banana oats:** green banana + Greek yoghurt + milk + oats + cinnamon

* **Fruit and ricotta:** green banana + ricotta + vanilla extract + crushed almonds + pepitas

* **Fruit smoothie:** banana starch + berries + milk + peanut butter.

Wholegrains: barley, buckwheat, rolled oats, pasta, rice, quinoa

These grains are all high in resistant starch, and are extremely versatile in salads and soups, as well as sides. See our guide on how to cook them (see pages 118–119) and our recipe section for ways to incorporate a variety of grains into your diet.

BUILD YOUR OWN: WHOLEGRAIN SALADS AND SOUPS

* **Lamb and barley salad:** barley + grilled lamb + feta + cos lettuce + cherry tomato + cucumber + lemon + pepper + roast almonds + mint + flat-leaf parsley

* **Salmon soba salad:** 100% buckwheat soba noodles + hot smoked salmon + spring onion + picked ginger + bok choy + soy sauce + mirin + sesame seeds

* **Tuna pasta salad:** wholemeal pasta + tuna + mozzarella + zucchini + cherry tomato + rocket + basil + lemon juice + olive oil

* **Japanese noodle soup:** 100% buckwheat soba noodles + soft-boiled egg + mushroom + bok choy/spinach + carrot + spring onion + ginger + garlic + clear broth (miso- or soy-based) + pickled veg + sesame seeds.

Cashew nuts

These tasty little nuts are high in resistant starch and make a great snack on the go. Eat them on their own, or add to stir-fries, curries and salads for crunch and texture. Cashew nuts pair well with chicken – try a quick stir-fry with vegetables and a small amount of sauce for flavour (see right).

WAYS WITH CASHEWS

* **Make a smoothie:** add cashews to your morning smoothie for a creamy texture

* **Meal topper**: lightly toast cashews over medium heat until golden. Top stir-fries, salads and soups

* **Chicken and cashew stir-fry:** chicken breast + cashews + green veg (bok choy, asparagus, broccolini) + ginger + soy sauce

* **Cashew and chickpea salad:** cashews + chickpeas + capsicum + carrot + spring onion + rocket + cucumber + lemon juice (Optional: pearl barley or freekeh + currants).

Legumes: beans, peas and lentils

Legumes are the 'multi-taskers' of the food pyramid. A great plant-based source of protein and carbohydrate, they are major providers of fibre and resistant starch, making them essential to a healthy gut diet. Also highly adaptable flavour carriers, legumes can be used whole in salads, wraps, curries, stews, pies and pasta dishes, or blended to create dips, patties and even breads. They are a key feature in many cuisines including Mexican, Indian, Nepalese and Middle Eastern. And let's not forget the humble green pea – a freezer staple, peas can be slipped into many meals for an extra fibre hit. See our section on cooking and preparing dried legumes (see pages 120–121). If you're in a rush, salt-reduced tinned legumes are a quick and easy alternative.

BUILD YOUR OWN: LEGUME LUNCHES

* **Hummus dip:** chickpeas + lemon juice + tahini + garlic + olive oil. Sprinkle with ground cumin, sumac or smoked paprika for extra flavour

* **Four-bean salad:** four-bean mix + lettuce + fennel + celery + corn + feta + dill + lemon juice + olive oil

* **Chicken and pea risotto:** rice + green peas + garlic + leek + mushroom + fennel + lemon zest

* **Beef and lentil soup:** beef + lentils + tomatoes + swede + turnip + onion + spinach + mushrooms

* **Moroccan bean and veg braise:** cannellini beans + onion + carrot + celery + swede + turnip + parsnip + bay leaves + toasted cumin + coriander seeds + sumac. Serve with white fish and tahini yoghurt.

Potatoes and sweet potatoes

Potatoes and sweet potatoes are some of the most well-known sources of resistant starch. The resistant starch content is known to increase when potatoes are roasted and cooled before eating. The heating (e.g. steaming or baking) and then cooling process produces a different type of resistant starch in potatoes, increasing the resistant starch content.

Any type of cooking process can be used, if the potatoes are cooled (e.g. in the fridge overnight) before consumption. (It is also fine to reheat them to eat: in fact, this can also increase the resistant starch content.)

PREP-AHEAD POTATOES

* **Roast veg:** roast potato + pumpkin + carrot + fennel + beetroot + sweet potato + zucchini + capsicum + anything else that you have in the fridge! Flavour with rosemary + fennel seeds + bay leaves + olive oil. Refrigerate and keep for up to a week for quick snacks, or for adding to salads with leafy greens and a dash of balsamic or red wine vinegar. Serve with pine nuts + pepitas

* **Sweet potato:** slice a large sweet potato into rounds and bake. Serve with your favourite toppings: think grated carrot + spinach + grated cheese + mashed avocado; or kidney beans + corn + avocado + lime salsa + cucumber + light sour cream.

Pumpernickel bread

Originating in Germany, pumpernickel is a dense loaf traditionally made of rye grains and fermented with sourdough starter. Top pumpernickel slices with a spread, a protein serve, and add your favourite salads and vegetables – see right for our favourite ideas.

BUILD YOUR OWN: LOAF TOPPERS

* **Try pumpernickel topped with:**
  - avocado + boiled egg + kimchi + baby spinach
  - light cream cheese + smoked salmon + capers + rocket + dill
  - wholegrain mustard + roast beef + roast beetroot + leafy greens
  - light cream cheese + cranberry + turkey + cucumber + lettuce

* **Pumpernickel crouton salad:** cubed toasted pumpernickel + avocado + red wine vinaigrette + chicken + basil and/or marjoram + tomato + capsicum + shallot.

PART THREE

THE recipes

THE CSIRO HEALTHY GUT RECIPES

Our recipes have been developed with your lifestyle and enjoyment at front of mind! Not only are our recipes packed with fibre and other nutrients, but they include a variety of core foods, exciting ingredients, a mixture of cooking methods, and cater to a range of dietary preferences.

We want you to use the recipes and meal plans in this book to their full potential to suit your, and your family's, lifestyle – whether that means following the recipe to a tee, adding your own flair, swapping ingredients here and there, or preparing meals in advance to freeze or refrigerate. You'll see that many of our recipes have options that leave the choice up to you. For example, with breads and cereals, we have suggested the best flavour combinations, but feel free to use what you have at home – sourdough bread can be swapped for wholegrain bread, or rice swapped for pearl barley. Similarly, milks and yoghurts can be dairy-based or lactose free, or from an alternative source. If you are using an alternative to cow's milk, be sure to choose a high-calcium option.

Eat a variety of grains, fruits, and vegetables each week. This will ensure that you consume different types of fibres – and fibre diversity is important. We have included several recipes with vegetarian protein sources, such as legumes and tofu – you'll notice that these portions are on the larger side! We have made sure that our vegetarian recipes include adequate protein, and as plant-based sources are less protein-rich than animal-based ingredients, this means the serves are larger in size. If the serves are too big, freeze the meals in portions so that you can easily grab what you need and reheat for a quick and healthy lunch or dinner on a busy day.

Fibre rating

Every recipe in this book has a fibre rating (see the key below). Use this information to choose which recipes to cook and eat throughout the week. For example, if you make two or three recipes from the book each day, it's fine to choose those that are lower in fibre because, all together, you can be sure you will eat enough fibre for the day. If you are only choosing one recipe from the book to prepare, however, pick one that is an excellent source of fibre.

You can take the same approach with packaged foods when reading labels. Items such as breads and cereals may have a statement on the package saying 'good source' or 'excellent source' of fibre. According to Australian and New Zealand food-labelling rules, these foods must have at least 4 grams of fibre per serve to be a good source, or 7 grams of fibre per serve to be an excellent source. Check the nutrition information panel on the package and choose foods that are higher sources of fibre.

We have also highlighted recipes that are a good source of resistant starch. Try to eat a few of these recipes each week, and on other days, snack on foods high in resistant starch, such as slightly unripe bananas, or handfuls of cashew nuts. You'll notice that we haven't listed the amount of resistant starch in the recipes. This is because the amount can vary according to growing conditions, processing methods, cooking time and temperature, as well as storage and reheating.

FIBRE RATING KEY

For every recipe in this book, you will find a fibre rating:

EXCELLENT SOURCE OF FIBRE

at least 7 g per serve

GOOD SOURCE OF FIBRE

at least 4 g per serve

CONTAINS FIBRE

at least 0.5 g per serve

EATING FOR A HEALTHY GUT

In summary, here are the key principles of the CSIRO Healthy Gut Diet:

 * Eat at least 25–30 g of total dietary fibre each day.

 * Choose foods that are higher in resistant starch (see page 26).

 * Add high-fibre foods to your diet slowly.

 * Drink plenty of water each day.

 * Limit highly processed foods.

 * Limit added salt and sugars.

 * Minimise alcohol.

 * Exercise regularly – this creates movement for the bowel.

DAILY MEAL PLAN: FIBRE FOR FAMILIES

Fibre is important for the whole family! It's best for children to eat the same healthy foods as the rest of the family. Choosing meals for the whole family might seem challenging at times, so here are some tips and meal ideas to keep everyone happy.

* Include the whole family in food choices and meal preparation, and scale down the kitchen activities based on children's abilities.

* School-aged children can pack their own lunch boxes – offer a range of healthy foods and allow them to choose from the options that you have provided.

 ## Breakfast

Quick oats: 30 g rolled or quick oats + 1 cup skim milk + 150 g berries

 ## Lunch

Pea falafels with brussels sprout slaw (page 155)

> ### TIP
>
> Making falafels is a great way to get children to participate in the kitchen — there are plenty of opportunities to practise measuring, mixing and moulding falafels into shape. Mix and match any salad vegetables from the fridge. Add to a roll or a wrap for an extra carbohydrate serve for active, growing bodies.

 Dinner

---

Sweet potatoes with spiced lamb
(page 193)

> ### TIP
>
> Packed with vegetables, minced meat and legumes, this is a wholesome and filling family favourite. Reduce the spices if you're cooking for sensitive taste buds, and let everyone at the table choose their own toppings.

 Snacks

---

Fresh fruit, such as an apple or a slightly unripe banana

1 cup veggie sticks (carrot, celery, cucumber, capsicum, snow peas) with **homemade tzatziki dip**

Daily units

Wholegrain high-fibre breads, cereals, legumes **3** ✳ Lean meat, fish, poultry, eggs, tofu, legumes **3** ✳ Fruit **2** ✳ Vegetables **5** ✳ Dairy **3** ✳ Healthy fats and oils **7** ✳ Fibre **49 g** ✳ Energy **7500 kJ**

DAILY MEAL PLAN: BUSY INDIVIDUALS

Planning and preparing meals and snacks in advance are key to healthy eating when you have a busy lifestyle. We have a selected a combination of meals that can be prepared in advance and taste great reheated – so you can make the most of leftovers, and save precious time by grabbing a quick and easy meal that you've already prepared, or a snack to eat on the run!

Breakfast

Overnight oats:
30 g rolled oats + ½ cup skim milk + 100 g natural yoghurt + 1 cup frozen berries

> **TIP**
>
> Make ahead of time and store in the fridge.

Lunch

Autumn radicchio and butter bean salad (page 147)

> **TIP**
>
> Make this in advance for 4 days of lunches! Keep the bread and dressing separate until ready to eat.

 # Dinner

---

Valentine's chicken (page 178)

TIP
Throw it in the oven and let it cook while you do other things … it will be ready before you know it.

 # Snacks

---

1 boiled egg

1 cup fruit salad (drained if store-bought)

Regular skim-milk latte

Daily units

Wholegrain high-fibre breads, cereals, legumes **3** ✳ Lean meat, fish, poultry, eggs, tofu, legumes **3** ✳ Fruit **2** ✳ Vegetables **5** ✳ Dairy **3** ✳ Healthy fats and oils **6** ✳ Fibre **58 g** ✳ Energy **7500 kJ**

DAILY MEAL PLAN: SHIFT WORKERS

Maintaining a healthy lifestyle as a shift worker is not without challenges. Pack meals and snacks as you would a 'day job', and try not to eat large meals before sleeping. You might like to swap breakfast and dinner times if you work overnight, to keep to a *semi* regular schedule and share meals with the family, and to save your lightest meal for just before bed. Foods that don't spoil, or that can be stored in a cooler bag and are transportable, can help keep you on track with your healthy-eating goals.

 Breakfast

Bondi sunrise thickie
(page 126)

TIP

This smoothie could also be a snack on your way to work, or mid-shift. Make two serves and keep one in the fridge for the next day.

 Lunch

Tuna salad with pumpernickel:
100 g tuna tinned in spring water
+ 4 cups salad vegetables
+ 1 slice pumpernickel bread
or ½ wholemeal wrap +
40 g cheddar or feta cheese

TIP

These ingredients will keep separately at room temperature or in a cooler bag for a couple of hours (except the cheese if it's a warm day). When you're ready to eat, mix it all together and eat as a salad.

 Dinner

Green seed bowl (page 170)

> **TIP**
>
> This is a light meal that can be prepared in advance, and doubles as a 'large breakfast' if your first meal of the day happens to be at dinner time. Keep the dressing separate, and boil eggs in advance (rather than using poached eggs) so that you can skip cooking when you're in a hurry.

 Snacks

Fresh fruit: something that travels well, such as an apple or a slightly unripe banana

Baby cucumber and carrot sticks

Small skim-milk latte

> **TIP**
>
> Apples, bananas and pears travel well, or pre-peel an orange and keep in a container to grab slices on the go.

Daily units

Wholegrain high-fibre breads, cereals, legumes **3** ✳ Lean meat, fish, poultry, eggs, tofu, legumes **3** ✳ Fruit **2** ✳ Vegetables **5** ✳ Dairy **3** ✳ Healthy fats and oils **6** ✳ Fibre **58 g** ✳ Energy **7500 kJ**

DAILY MEAL PLAN: OLDER ADULTS

As we get older, many of us like to keep things simple, while still getting all the nutrients we need to maintain strength and vitality. We have chosen some easy, nutrient-rich recipes to promote healthy ageing, to keep you active and on your feet.

 **Breakfast**

Spinach omelette: 2 eggs + ½ cup milk + ½ cup grated cheese + 1 cup baby spinach + 1 slice wholegrain toast

TIP
Start the day with a great source of protein and calcium for healthy bones and muscles. Limit eggs to no more than 7 per week if you have cardiovascular disease or type 2 diabetes.

 **Lunch**

Lentil nicoise salad (page 146)

TIP
A twist on a favourite, this budget-friendly salad is easy to prepare and can be stored in the fridge for leftovers. If you have eggs for breakfast, remove the eggs from this dish.

 Dinner

Pork with celeriac and white bean purée (page 184)

TIP
This dish goes well with any vegetables — you can use anything you have at home.

 Snacks

Banana bowls (page 212)

1 cup berries

TIP
Choose calcium-enriched dairy sources.

Daily units

Wholegrain high-fibre breads, cereals, legumes **3** ✳ Lean meat, fish, poultry, eggs, tofu, legumes **3** ✳ Fruit **2** ✳ Vegetables **5** ✳ Dairy **3** ✳ Healthy fats and oils **6** ✳ Fibre **50 g** ✳ Energy **7500 kJ**

PREPARING AND COOKING GRAINS

1 RINSE

Rinse the grains under cool running water and remove any stones or debris.

2 SOAK (OPTIONAL)

You may wish to soak your grains before cooking. Place them in a large bowl and cover generously with cold water. Add a dash of apple cider vinegar or a squeeze of lemon juice and mix to combine. Please note that if you soak your grains, they may cook more quickly than the times indicated in the table opposite. Keep an eye on them as they cook, tasting regularly to see how soft they are.

3 COOK

When you are ready to cook, add the grains and fresh water to a saucepan and bring to the boil. Reduce to a simmer and cook, covered, for the time listed in the table opposite. Once cooked, remove the pan from the heat, keeping the lid on, and set aside for 15 minutes to allow the grains to steam. Fluff with a fork before serving.

4 STORE

Once you've cooked the grains, they will keep in an airtight container in the fridge for 3–5 days. Alternatively, divide among containers and freeze for up to 6 months.

Grain cooking times

1 CUP GRAINS	ADD WATER	COOKING TIME	YIELD
pearl barley	2 cups	45–60 minutes	4 cups (760 g)
quinoa	2 cups	12–15 minutes	3 cups (360 g)
rice (brown)	2½ cups	25–45 minutes	3 cups (555 g)
rice (white)	2 cups	10–12 minutes	2¾ cups (510 g)

PREPARING AND COOKING DRIED LEGUMES

BEFORE YOU START

Make sure you start with fresh legumes, as those that have been stored for more than 12 months or in unfavourable conditions may never soften. The best age is from harvest to 4 months old. Older legumes will look dull and darker in colour, and have more cracked skins. They will also have declining nutrient levels.

1 RINSE

Rinse the legumes under cool running water and remove any stones or debris.

2 SOAK

Soaking legumes reduces their cooking time, allows the beans to cook more evenly and reduces flatulence-related substances in the legumes so they are easier to digest. These substances dissolve into the soaking water and are reduced when the soaking water is drained and replaced with fresh water. Place the legumes in a large bowl and cover generously with cold water. Soak for the time outlined in the table opposite. They are ready when they are uniformly tender and have doubled or more in size. Refer to the maximum soaking times in the table. If you plan to soak them for longer, put the bowl in the fridge so the legumes don't spoil. There is a 'quick soak' option if you are short on time. Just put the legumes in a saucepan, cover with water and bring to the boil, then cover the pan and turn off the heat. Let them sit for at least 30 minutes, then drain and go from there.

3 RINSE AGAIN

Drain the soaked legumes in a colander and rinse under cool running water.

4 COOK

Add the legumes to a pan and cover with at least 6 cm of water. Bring to the boil, then reduce the heat and simmer until tender, skimming off any foam that forms on the surface. Don't cook legumes on a strong boil, as they will cook unevenly and the skins will burst.

Simmer for the time specified in the table below, but do note that times can vary, so taste the legumes every now and then until they are cooked through and tender to the bite. Drain, and they're ready to use.

If you are planning to add the legumes to a soup or stew, it's best to undercook them by 10–15 minutes and let them finish cooking in your recipe. This will stop them turning mushy.

5 STORE

Once you've cooked the legumes, they will keep in an airtight container in the fridge for 3–5 days. Alternatively, separate into containers and freeze for up to 6 months.

Legume cooking times

1 CUP LEGUMES	SOAKING TIME	COOKING TIME	YIELD
adzuki beans	8–10 hours	45–55 minutes	3 cups (465 g)
black beans	8–10 hours	1–1½ hours	2¼ cups (360 g)
black-eyed peas	8–10 hours	1 hour	2 cups (320 g)
brown lentils	no soaking required	20–25 minutes	2¼ cups (350 g)
butter beans	8–10 hours	45–60 minutes	2 cups (320 g)
cannellini beans	8–10 hours	45 minutes	2½ cups (400 g)
chickpeas	12 hours	1–2 hours	2 cups (320 g)
French (puy) lentils	no soaking required	25–30 minutes	2 cups (310 g)
kidney beans	8–10 hours	1 hour	2¼ cups (360 g)
mung beans	8–10 hours	1 hour	2 cups (300 g)
navy beans	8–10 hours	45–60 minutes	2⅔ cups (425 g)
pinto beans	no soaking required	1–1½ hours	2⅔ cups (440 g)
soy beans	10–12 hours	3–4 hours	3 cups (480 g)
yellow split peas	no soaking required	45–60 minutes	2 cups (300 g)

BREAKFAST

Smoothies

Blueberry
pancake batter
smoothie
PAGE 126

Bondi sunrise
thickie
PAGE 126

TIP

You can choose from almond, macadamia, rice, oat or cow's milk for these smoothies. When choosing dairy-free milks, read the label and make sure they have added calcium.

Pear and oat shake
PAGE 127

Tahini banana blizzard
PAGE 127

Smoothies

Blueberry pancake batter smoothie

SERVES: 2 **PREP:** 5 MINS

12g
TOTAL FIBRE

★★★
FIBRE RATING

✓
RESISTANT STARCH

1 medium banana, chopped and frozen

1 cup (155 g) fresh or frozen blueberries

3 tablespoons reduced-fat Greek-style yoghurt

1 teaspoon vanilla extract

¾ cup (185 ml) almond milk

⅔ cup (100 g) quinoa flakes

2 teaspoons cashew butter

1½ tablespoons chia seeds

Place all the ingredients in a blender and blend on high until smooth.

Add 3 tablespoons water if you prefer a thinner consistency, and blitz again.

Pour into two glasses and serve.

> ### TIP
> You can replace the quinoa flakes with rolled oats, if you like.

Wholegrain high-fibre breads, cereals and legumes **1** ✳ Lean meat, fish, poultry, eggs, tofu and legumes **0** ✳ Fruit **1** ✳ Vegetables **0** ✳ Dairy **0.5** ✳ Healthy fats and oils **2**

Bondi sunrise thickie

SERVES: 2 **PREP:** 5 MINS

11g
TOTAL FIBRE

★★★
FIBRE RATING

1½ cups (280 g) diced mango, frozen

⅔ cup (100 g) quinoa flakes

¼ teaspoon ground turmeric

1½ cups (375 ml) macadamia milk

2 teaspoons cashew butter (or any nut butter)

2 teaspoons chia seeds

To serve

1 teaspoon coconut flakes

1 teaspoon chia seeds

Place all the ingredients in a blender and blend on high until smooth.

Pour into two glasses and finish with the coconut flakes and chia seeds to serve.

> ### TIP
> If you haven't frozen your banana in advance, add 1 cup ice cubes to ensure the smoothie is cold.

Wholegrain high-fibre breads, cereals and legumes **1** ✳ Lean meat, fish, poultry, eggs, tofu and legumes **0** ✳ Fruit **1** ✳ Vegetables **0** ✳ Dairy **1** ✳ Healthy fats and oils **2**

Pear and oat shake

SERVES: 2 **PREP:** 5 MINS

8g	★★	✓
TOTAL FIBRE	FIBRE RATING	RESISTANT STARCH

½ medium banana, chopped and frozen

1 small pear, chopped and frozen

pinch of ground cardamom

¼ teaspoon ground cinnamon

3 tablespoons reduced-fat natural yoghurt

1 cup (250 ml) oat milk

²/₃ cup (65 g) rolled oats

3 teaspoons almond butter

2 teaspoons unsalted roasted almonds, roughly chopped

Place all the ingredients except the chopped almonds in a blender and blitz on high until smooth.

Pour into two glasses, top with the almonds and serve.

Tahini banana blizzard

SERVES: 2 **PREP:** 5 MINS

6g	★★	✓
TOTAL FIBRE	FIBRE RATING	RESISTANT STARCH

2 medium bananas, chopped and frozen

1 cup (250 ml) almond milk

½ teaspoon ground cinnamon

20 g buckwheat flour

⅓ cup (35 g) rolled oats

1 tablespoon unhulled tahini

Place all the ingredients in a blender and blend on high until smooth.

Add 2–3 tablespoons water if you prefer a thinner consistency, and blitz again.

Pour into two glasses and serve.

TIP

To turn this into an espresso banana blizzard, add a cooled shot of coffee.

Wholegrain high-fibre breads, cereals and legumes **1** ❋
Lean meat, fish, poultry, eggs, tofu and legumes **0** ❋ Fruit **1**
❋ Vegetables **0** ❋ Dairy **1** ❋ Healthy fats and oils **2**

Wholegrain high-fibre breads, cereals and legumes **1** ❋
Lean meat, fish, poultry, eggs, tofu and legumes **0** ❋ Fruit **1**
❋ Vegetables **0** ❋ Dairy **0.5** ❋ Healthy fats and oils **2**

Buckwheat crepes with salmon

3g
TOTAL
FIBRE

★
FIBRE
RATING

160 g mozzarella, grated

1 tablespoon capers, rinsed

150 g hot smoked salmon

1 tablespoon horseradish cream

2 cups (60 g) watercress sprigs

3 tablespoons unsalted roasted almonds, roughly chopped

1 teaspoon extra virgin olive oil

lemon wedges, to serve (optional)

Buckwheat crepes

80 g buckwheat flour

1 large free-range egg

2 teaspoons extra virgin olive oil

1. To make the buckwheat crepe batter, place the flour in a large bowl, crack in the egg and add 1 cup (250 ml) water. Mix well to form a thin, smooth batter. Set aside to rest for at least 1 hour, but preferably for 2 hours before cooking.

2. Heat ½ teaspoon olive oil in a large non-stick frying pan over medium heat. Pour in one-quarter of the batter and swirl the pan to cover the base, making a thin crepe. Place one-quarter of the mozzarella, capers and smoked salmon in the middle. Continue to cook for 4–6 minutes until the crepe is browned and crispy on the bottom and the cheese has melted.

3. Fold over the crepe and transfer to a plate. Cover to keep warm, then repeat with the remaining batter, mozzarella, capers and salmon to make four crepes.

4. Serve the crepes with the horseradish cream, watercress and almonds. Finish with a light drizzle of olive oil, a pinch of freshly ground black pepper and a lemon wedge for squeezing over, if you like.

Wholegrain high-fibre breads, cereals and legumes **1** ✳ Lean meat, fish, poultry, eggs, tofu and legumes **0.5** ✳ Fruit **0** ✳ Vegetables **0.5** ✳ Dairy **1** ✳ Healthy fats and oils **2**

Toast Toppers

Open sesame

SERVES: 2 **PREP:** 5 MINS **COOK:** 5 MINS

5g TOTAL FIBRE	★★ FIBRE RATING

3 tablespoons ripe avocado

1 tablespoon reduced-fat Greek-style yoghurt

½ teaspoon sesame oil

2 thin slices wholemeal bread, toasted

½ teaspoon sesame seeds

3 tablespoons coriander leaves

Place the avocado, yoghurt, sesame oil and a pinch of freshly ground black pepper in a bowl and mash to combine.

Spread the avocado mixture over the toast, top with sesame seeds and coriander leaves and serve.

> ### TIP
>
> Choose from sourdough, rye, wholemeal, pumperknickel or gluten-free bread for these toast-topper recipes.

Wholegrain high-fibre breads, cereals and legumes **1** ☀
Lean meat, fish, poultry, eggs, tofu and legumes **0** ☀
Fruit **0** ☀ Vegetables **0** ☀ Dairy **<0.5** ☀ Healthy fats and oils **2**

The Scandi

SERVES: 2 **PREP:** 10 MINS **COOK:** 10 MINS

3g TOTAL FIBRE	★ FIBRE RATING	√ RESISTANT STARCH

2 free-range eggs

1 tablespoon whole-egg mayonnaise

1 teaspoon Dijon mustard

2 teaspoons extra virgin olive oil

2 thin slices rye bread, toasted

2 radishes, thinly sliced

2 teaspoons finely chopped dill

Half-fill a large saucepan with water and bring to the boil over medium–high heat. Add the eggs and cook for 9 minutes, then remove with a slotted spoon and plunge into cold water to stop them cooking. When cool enough to handle, peel and finely chop the eggs.

Gently combine the chopped egg, mayonnaise, mustard, olive oil and a pinch of freshly ground black pepper in a bowl.

Spread the egg mixture on the toast, top with the radish and dill and serve.

Wholegrain high-fibre breads, cereals and legumes **1** ☀
Lean meat, fish, poultry, eggs, tofu and legumes **0.5** ☀
Fruit **0** ☀ Vegetables **0** ☀ Dairy **0** ☀ Healthy fats and oils **2**

Open sesame

The Scandi

131

Salmon, avo and ricotta

SERVES: 2 **PREP:** 5 MINS
COOK: 5 MINS

2g TOTAL FIBRE   ★ FIBRE RATING

½ medium avocado

3 tablespoons reduced-fat fresh ricotta

juice of ½ lemon

pinch of dried chilli flakes, plus extra to serve

2 slices pumpernickel bread, toasted

1 cup (60 g) alfalfa sprouts

100 g smoked salmon

½ small red onion, thinly sliced

lemon wedge, to serve (optional)

Place the avocado, ricotta, lemon juice and chilli flakes in a bowl, season with freshly ground black pepper and mash to combine.

Spread the avocado mixture over the toast and top with the alfalfa sprouts, smoked salmon and red onion. Finish with a sprinkling of extra chilli flakes and serve immediately with lemon for squeezing over, if you like.

Wholegrain high-fibre breads, cereals and legumes 1 ⁂ Lean meat, fish, poultry, eggs, tofu and legumes 0 ⁂ Fruit 0 ⁂ Vegetables 0.5 ⁂ Dairy 0.5 ⁂ Healthy fats and oils 2

Kimchi coriander

SERVES: 2 **PREP:** 5 MINS
COOK: 5 MINS

2g TOTAL FIBRE   ★ FIBRE RATING

3 tablespoons reduced-fat cream cheese

2 thin slices sourdough bread, toasted

½ cup (70 g) Kimchi (see page 60)

3 tablespoons coriander leaves

1 tablespoon unsalted roasted peanuts, roughly chopped

2 teaspoons extra virgin olive oil

Spread the cream cheese across the toast. Top with the kimchi, coriander leaves and peanuts.

Drizzle over the olive oil and finish with a good pinch of freshly ground black pepper.

Wholegrain high-fibre breads, cereals and legumes 1 ⁂ Lean meat, fish, poultry, eggs, tofu and legumes 0 ⁂ Fruit 0 ⁂ Vegetables 0.5 ⁂ Dairy 0.5 ⁂ Healthy fats and oils 2

Tomato and peach

SERVES: 2 **PREP:** 10 MINS
COOK: 5 MINS

3g TOTAL FIBRE   ★ FIBRE RATING

6 cherry tomatoes, sliced

1 small peach, sliced

40 g reduced-fat goat's feta, crumbled

1 tablespoon extra virgin olive oil

2 thin slices sourdough bread, toasted

mint leaves, to serve

Place the tomato, peach and feta in a bowl. Add 2 teaspoons olive oil and a pinch of freshly ground black pepper and gently toss to combine.

Drizzle the remaining olive oil over the toast and top with the tomato mixture. Sprinkle with mint leaves and serve.

Wholegrain high-fibre breads, cereals and legumes 1 ⁂ Lean meat, fish, poultry, eggs, tofu and legumes 0 ⁂ Fruit 0.5 ⁂ Vegetables 0.5 ⁂ Dairy 0.5 ⁂ Healthy fats and oils 2

Kimchi coriander

Tomato and
peach

Salmon, avo and
ricotta

Banana nut granola

8g
TOTAL
FIBRE

★★★
FIBRE
RATING

✓
RESISTANT
STARCH

1 medium banana

1⅔ cups (165 g) rolled oats

½ cup (100 g) raw buckwheat groats

2 tablespoons walnuts

2 tablespoons hazelnuts,
roughly chopped

1½ tablespoons extra virgin olive oil

2 teaspoons ground cinnamon

2 teaspoons vanilla extract

To serve

1½ cups (375 g) reduced-fat natural
yoghurt

250 g raspberries

1. Preheat the oven to 180°C (160°C fan-forced) and line a large baking tray with baking paper.
2. Mash the banana in a large bowl, then add the remaining granola ingredients and mix well (the most effective way to do this is with your hands).
3. Spread out the granola on the prepared tray, leaving some of it in chunks. Bake for 15 minutes, then remove from the oven and toss. Return to the oven for another 8–10 minutes, until nicely golden.
4. Allow to cool on the tray, then serve with the yoghurt and raspberries.
5. Store any leftover granola in an airtight container for up to 1 week.

TIPS

* This is a great recipe to make on the weekend; store in an airtight container and enjoy for weekday breakfasts.
* To make this portable, spoon the yoghurt into a jar and top with the granola and raspberries. Combine before eating.
* You can also enjoy this as cereal, using ½ cup (125 ml) milk per serve, in place of the yoghurt.

Wholegrain high-fibre breads, legumes and cereals **1** ✳ Lean meat, fish, poultry, eggs, tofu and legumes **0** ✳
Fruit **0.5** ✳ Vegetables **0** ✳ Dairy **0.5** ✳ Healthy fats and oils **2**

SERVES: 2 **PREP:** 10 MINS **COOK:** 10 MINS

Leek and parmesan omelette

5g
TOTAL
FIBRE

FIBRE
RATING

1 tablespoon extra virgin olive oil

1 small leek, white part only, thinly sliced

1 garlic clove, minced

1½ tablespoons skim milk

2 large free-range eggs, separated

1 tablespoon finely chopped dill, plus extra to serve

30 g parmesan, grated

2 thin slices wholemeal bread, toasted

1. Preheat the oven grill to high.
2. Heat 3 teaspoons olive oil in a large frying pan over medium heat. Add the leek and garlic and cook, stirring, for 3–4 minutes until tender. Remove and set aside.
3. In a large bowl, whisk together the milk, egg yolks, dill and half the parmesan.
4. In another clean bowl, whisk the egg whites until soft peaks form, then gently fold into the egg yolk mixture.
5. Place the frying pan back over medium heat, pour in the egg mixture and tilt to cover the base of the pan. Cook for 1–2 minutes, until the underside is golden. Scatter over the leek and garlic mixture and the remaining parmesan, then place under the grill for about 1 minute until the top is lightly golden.
6. Using a spatula, fold the omelette in half, then slice in half and place on two plates. Scatter over some extra dill, season with freshly ground black pepper and drizzle over the remaining olive oil. Serve with the wholemeal toast.

Wholegrain high-fibre breads, legumes and cereals **1** ✳ Lean meat, fish, poultry, eggs, tofu and legumes **0.5** ✳ Fruit **0** ✳ Vegetables **0.5** ✳ Dairy **0.5** ✳ Healthy fats and oils **2**

Lush Yoghurt Bowls

Golden blackberry

SERVES: 2 **PREP:** 5 MINS

7g
TOTAL FIBRE

★★★
FIBRE RATING

1½ cups (375 g) reduced-fat natural yoghurt

¼ teaspoon ground turmeric, plus extra to sprinkle

½ teaspoon ground cinnamon, plus extra to sprinkle

½ teaspoon vanilla extract

⅔ cup (20 g) puffed rice

¾ cup (100 g) blackberries, fresh or frozen

1 tablespoon unhulled tahini

Mix together the yoghurt, turmeric, cinnamon and vanilla in a bowl.

Divide between two bowls and top with the puffed rice, blackberries and a dollop of tahini.

TIPS

* If you can't find blackberries, replace with fresh or frozen blueberries.
* To prep the night before, layer everything except the puffed rice in a jar. Top with the puffed rice just before serving.

Wholegrain high-fibre breads, cereals and legumes **1**
Lean meat, fish, poultry, eggs, tofu and legumes **0**　Fruit
0.5　Vegetables **0**　Dairy **1**　Healthy fats and oils **2**

Apple pie

SERVES: 2 **PREP:** 5 MINS

6g
TOTAL FIBRE

★★
FIBRE RATING

✓
RESISTANT STARCH

1½ cups (375 g) reduced-fat natural yoghurt

1 teaspoon ground cinnamon

pinch of freshly grated nutmeg

1 teaspoon vanilla extract

⅔ cup (65 g) quick oats

1 small red apple, cored and thinly sliced

3 teaspoons almond butter

2 teaspoons shredded coconut

In a bowl, mix the yoghurt with the cinnamon, nutmeg and vanilla.

Divide between two bowls. Top with the oats, apple, almond butter and coconut. Stir to combine and serve.

TIPS

* If you don't have almond butter, use peanut butter instead.
* For a portable breakfast, simply layer all the ingredients in a jar.

Wholegrain high fibre breads, cereals and legumes **1**
Lean meat, fish, poultry, eggs, tofu and legumes **0**　Fruit
0.5　Vegetables **0**　Dairy **1**　Healthy fats and oils **2**

Peanut butter jelly

SERVES: 2 **PREP:** 5 MINS, PLUS STANDING

13g
TOTAL
FIBRE

★★★
FIBRE
RATING

1½ cups (375 g) reduced-fat natural yoghurt

2 teaspoons chia seeds

⅔ cup (100 g) quinoa flakes

3 teaspoons crunchy peanut butter (no added sugar or salt)

250 g raspberries, lightly mashed (or use frozen berries, thawed)

Combine the yoghurt, chia seeds, quinoa flakes and ²/₃ cup (170 ml) water in a bowl. Set aside for 20–30 minutes to allow the chia seeds to absorb the liquid.

Divide the yoghurt mixture between two bowls and top with a dollop of peanut butter and the raspberries.

> ## TIP
>
> Prep this the night before by adding all the ingredients to a jar – the chia seeds will absorb the liquid and you'll have a delicious breakfast for the morning.

Wholegrain high-fibre breads, cereals and legumes **1**
Lean meat, fish, poultry, eggs, tofu and legumes **0**　Fruit
1　Vegetables **0**　Dairy **1**　Healthy fats and oils **2**

Crispy chilli eggs

4g
TOTAL
FIBRE

FIBRE
RATING

2 teaspoons extra virgin olive oil

2 spring onions, thinly sliced

1 cup (90 g) sugar snap peas, trimmed and thinly sliced

2 large free-range eggs

pinch of ground turmeric

pinch of sweet paprika

pinch of dried chilli flakes, plus extra to serve (optional)

2 slices wholemeal bread

3 tablespoons reduced-fat feta, crumbled

2 tablespoons mashed avocado

1. Heat the olive oil in a large frying pan over medium–high heat. Add the spring onion and cook for 1 minute or until starting to soften. Add the sugar snaps and toss for another 30 seconds until starting to soften.

2. Make two spaces and crack in the eggs. Sprinkle the turmeric, paprika and chilli flakes over the white edges of the eggs. Cook for 3–4 minutes, until the egg whites are set but the yolks are still soft.

3. Meanwhile, toast the bread. Serve the eggs with the feta, avocado and toast, finishing with a good grinding of black pepper and extra chilli, if you like.

Wholegrain high-fibre breads, cereals and legumes **1** ✳ Lean meat, fish, poultry, eggs, tofu and legumes **0.5** ✳ Fruit **0** ✳ Vegetables **0.5** ✳ Dairy **0.5** ✳ Healthy fats and oils **2**

LUNCH

Broccoli pesto pasta

21g
TOTAL
FIBRE

★★★
FIBRE
RATING

√
RESISTANT
STARCH

150 g low-GI wholemeal pasta

3 teaspoons extra virgin olive oil

1 large onion, finely chopped

1 large zucchini, finely diced

1 cup (155 g) frozen peas

4 cups (60 g) chopped cavolo nero
or kale

juice of ½ lemon

200 g drained tinned tuna
in spring water

40 g parmesan, shaved

Broccoli pesto

1 head broccoli, florets and stem
chopped into 1–2 cm pieces

2½ tablespoons extra virgin olive oil

2 garlic cloves, unpeeled

2 tablespoons walnuts

1 bunch basil, leaves picked

1 bunch coriander, stems and leaves
roughly chopped

60 g parmesan, grated

1. Preheat the oven to 180°C (160°C fan-forced).
2. To start the pesto, scatter the broccoli over a large baking tray and drizzle with 1 teaspoon olive oil. Add the garlic cloves, then place in the oven and roast for 20 minutes. Scatter over the walnuts and roast for a further 5 minutes, or until the broccoli is tender and lightly charred and the walnuts are golden brown.
3. Meanwhile, cook the pasta according to the packet instructions, then drain and set aside.
4. Heat the olive oil in a large frying pan over medium heat. Add the onion and zucchini and cook for 8–10 minutes until tender. Add the peas and cavolo nero or kale and cook for 2 minutes, until the peas have thawed and the cavolo nero or kale has wilted. Remove from the heat while you finish the pesto.
5. Tip the roasted broccoli and walnuts into a food processor and squeeze in the flesh from the garlic cloves. Add the remaining olive oil, basil, coriander and parmesan and blitz to form a chunky paste.
6. Add the pesto, drained pasta and lemon juice to the frying pan and toss through the vegetable mixture to coat. Season with black pepper and add the tuna, then gently toss again.
7. Divide evenly among four bowls, sprinkle over the parmesan and serve.

TIP

To make this vegetarian, omit the tuna and mash 1 boiled egg through each bowl of pasta instead.

Wholegrain high-fibre breads, cereals and legumes **2** ✳ Lean meat, fish, poultry, eggs, tofu and legumes **0.5** ✳ Fruit **0**
✳ Vegetables **2** ✳ Dairy **0.5** ✳ Healthy fats and oils **4**

Golden lentil kitchari

20 g
TOTAL
FIBRE

★★★
FIBRE
RATING

✓
RESISTANT
STARCH

3 tablespoons extra virgin olive oil

2 onions, diced

2 large carrots, diced

1 large zucchini, diced

4 garlic cloves, minced

1 tablespoon minced ginger

1 tablespoon ground cumin

1 tablespoon ground coriander

2 teaspoons ground turmeric

2 cups (400 g) moong dal, soaked for 6–8 hours, drained (see tips)

¾ cup (150 g) basmati rice

1 litre salt-reduced vegetable stock

½ head cauliflower, roughly chopped

To serve

1 cup coriander leaves

½ teaspoon dried chilli flakes

1 cup (250 g) reduced-fat natural yoghurt

2 tablespoons unsalted roasted almonds

1. Heat the olive oil in a large (about 7 litre) saucepan or stockpot over medium heat. Add the onion, carrot and zucchini and cook, stirring, for 15 minutes, until the veggies are very tender. Add the garlic, ginger, cumin, ground coriander and turmeric and cook for another 2 minutes until fragrant.

2. Add the moong dal and rice and stir through the spiced vegetables. Add the stock and 2 cups (500 ml) water. Reduce the heat to medium–low and cook, stirring regularly, for 25 minutes. Keep an eye on it and add more water as needed to maintain a loose porridge-like consistency; you may need anything from 2 cups (500 ml) to 1 litre of water.

3. Add the cauliflower and cook for another 10 minutes, or until the cauliflower is cooked through, and the moong dal and rice have broken down and are tender to the bite.

4. Divide the kitchari among four bowls. Top with coriander leaves, chilli flakes, yoghurt and almonds and serve.

TIPS

* Moong dal is also known as mung dal or split yellow mung beans. You can buy it in health-food stores or bulk-food stores, but if you can't find it use red lentils instead. It's important that you soak the moong dal beforehand to reduce the cooking time and make the meal easier to digest.
* Store any leftover kitchari in an airtight container in the fridge for up to 3 days, or in the freezer for up to 3 months.

Wholegrain high-fibre breads, cereals and legumes 1 ✳ Lean meat, fish, poultry, eggs, tofu and legumes 1 ✳ Fruit 0 ✳ Vegetables 2.5 ✳ Dairy <0.5 ✳ Healthy fats and oils 4

Really Good Salads

Lentil nicoise salad

15 g	★★★	✓
TOTAL FIBRE	FIBRE RATING	RESISTANT STARCH

SERVES: 4 **PREP:** 15 MINS **COOK:** 15 MINS

4 large free-range eggs

4 large kipfler potatoes (600 g), cut into wedges

450 g green beans, trimmed and sliced

2 tablespoons walnuts

300 g cooked French (puy) lentils (see pages 120–121)

250 g cherry tomatoes, halved

1 bunch radishes, bulbs thinly sliced

1 small red onion, thinly sliced

6 cups (270 g) rocket

1 tablespoon capers, rinsed

3 tablespoons roughly chopped dill

Mustard dressing

2 tablespoons Dijon mustard

3 tablespoons extra virgin olive oil

juice of 1 lemon

1. Fill a large saucepan with water and bring to the boil. Add the eggs (give the shells a wipe, if necessary) and potato wedges and cook for exactly 8 minutes. Remove the eggs with a slotted spoon and plunge into cold water to stop them cooking. Add the green beans to the boiling water and cook for another 2 minutes or until the potato is soft when pierced with a knife and the beans are lightly blanched, but still have some crunch. Drain and set aside.

2. Meanwhile, to make the dressing, place all the ingredients in a bowl, add 2 tablespoons water and a pinch of freshly ground black pepper and whisk to combine.

3. Crumble the walnuts into a frying pan over medium heat and cook, tossing regularly, for 3–4 minutes until toasted and lightly golden.

4. Place the lentils, tomato, radish, onion, rocket, capers, dill, walnuts and the cooked potato and green beans in a large bowl. Drizzle over the mustard dressing and lightly toss to combine and coat.

5. Divide the salad among four bowls. Peel the eggs and cut in half lengthways, then place two halves on each salad and serve.

TIP

If you don't have puy lentils prepared, you can use 1½ x 400 g tins of brown lentils instead.

Wholegrain high-fibre breads, cereals and legumes 1 ✳ Lean meat, fish, poultry, eggs, tofu and legumes 1 ✳ Fruit 0 ✳ Vegetables 2.5 ✳ Dairy 0 ✳ Healthy fats and oils 4

Autumn radicchio and butter bean salad

14g
TOTAL
FIBRE

FIBRE
RATING

RESISTANT
STARCH

SERVES: 4 **PREP:** 20 MINS **COOK:** 25 MINS

1 small head cauliflower, cut into florets

2 teaspoons extra virgin olive oil

2 teaspoons ground coriander

3 tablespoons unsalted skinned hazelnuts, roughly chopped

2 thin slices sourdough bread, torn into small pieces

300 g cooked butter beans (see pages 120–121) or drained and rinsed tinned butter beans

1 head radicchio, leaves roughly torn

1 bunch radishes, thinly sliced

1 large carrot, shredded

1 medium blood orange (or regular orange), sliced into segments

10 green olives, pitted and sliced

1½ cups (220 g) cooked barley (see pages 118–119)

80 g parmesan, grated

Dressing

1 tablespoon Dijon mustard

2 tablespoons extra virgin olive oil

1 tablespoon apple cider vinegar

1. Preheat the oven to 180°C (160°C fan-forced).
2. Place the cauliflower florets in a large baking tray, drizzle over olive oil and ground coriander and toss to coat. Spread it out evenly, then place in the middle of the oven and roast for 25 minutes, or until tender and crisp on the edges.
3. Meanwhile, spread out the hazelnuts and sourdough on another large baking tray. Place in the top half of the oven and bake for 10 minutes, until lightly golden. Remove from the oven and set aside.
4. To make the dressing, place all the ingredients in a jar and shake to combine.
5. Place the warm cauliflower, butter beans, radicchio, radish, carrot, orange, olives, barley, parmesan and half the toasted hazelnuts and sourdough in a large bowl. Pour over the dressing and toss to combine.
6. Divide the salad among four bowls and top with the remaining hazelnuts and sourdough.

Wholegrain high fibre breads, cereals and legumes 1 ✳ Lean meat, fish, poultry, eggs, tofu and legumes **0.5** ✳ Fruit **0.5** ✳ Vegetables **2.5** ✳ Dairy **0** ✳ Healthy fats and oils **4**

Cauliflower waldorf

SERVES: 4 **PREP:** 15 MINS **COOK:** 5 MINS

9g
TOTAL FIBRE

★★★
FIBRE RATING

½ small head cauliflower

1 baby fennel bulb, trimmed

1 medium green apple

4 celery sticks

2 heads witlof (endive)

400 g store-bought roasted chicken, shredded, skin and bones discarded

3 tablespoons walnuts

4 thin slices rye bread, toasted and cut into triangles

Dressing

3 tablespoons whole-egg mayonnaise

3 tablespoons reduced-fat Greek-style yoghurt

1 tablespoon extra virgin olive oil

juice of ½ lemon

1. Push the cauliflower through a thin slicing attachment on your food processor, use a mandoline or simply finely shred it with a sharp knife. Shred the fennel, green apple, celery and witlof in the same way. Place in a large bowl, add the shredded chicken and toss to combine.

2. To make the dressing, mix together all the ingredients in a small bowl. Add 1–2 tablespoons water to thin it out, then pour the dressing over the salad and toss to coat well.

3. Heat a large frying pan over medium heat. Crush the walnuts in your hand and add to the pan, then cook, tossing, for 2–3 minutes until golden brown.

4. Divide the salad among four bowls. Top with the walnuts and freshly ground black pepper, and serve with toasted rye bread triangles.

Wholegrain high-fibre breads, cereals and legumes 1 ✳ Lean meat, fish, poultry, eggs, tofu and legumes 1 ✳ Fruit <0.5 ✳ Vegetables 2.5 ✳ Dairy 0 ✳ Healthy fats and oils 4

The best tuna salad

SERVES: 4 **PREP:** 15 MINS **COOK:** 5 MINS

8g
TOTAL
FIBRE

★★
FIBRE
RATING

√
RESISTANT
STARCH

1 tablespoon poppy seeds

2 tablespoons sunflower seeds

1 small iceberg lettuce, shredded

2 Lebanese cucumbers, halved lengthways, thinly sliced into half moons

150 g snow peas, trimmed

80 g reduced-fat feta, crumbled

1 small avocado, diced

2 cups coriander leaves

2 cups (370 g) cooked white or brown rice (see pages 118–119)

380 g tinned tuna in spring water, drained

Dressing

juice of 1 lemon

1 tablespoon whole-egg mayonnaise

2 teaspoons extra virgin olive oil

1. Heat a large frying pan over medium heat, add the poppy seeds and sunflower seeds and toast, tossing, for 3–4 minutes until the sunflower seeds are golden. Using a mortar and pestle, grind until the seeds resemble a coarse almond meal. Set aside.

2. To make the dressing, place the lemon juice, mayonnaise, olive oil and a pinch of freshly ground black pepper in a jar and shake to combine.

3. Combine the lettuce, cucumber, snow peas, feta, avocado and coriander in a large bowl. Pour over the dressing and toss to coat.

4. Divide the rice evenly among four bowls, add the salad and gently combine. Flake the tuna over the top and finish with the toasted seed mixture.

TIPS

* This recipe is a delicious way to use up any left-over cooked rice, a great source of resistant starch.
* To prep ahead, you can store the salad in the fridge for 3–4 days. Keep the dressing, tuna, rice and toasted seeds separate and add just before serving.

Wholegrain high-fibre breads, cereals and legumes 1
* Lean meat, fish, poultry, eggs, tofu and legumes 1
* Fruit 0 * Vegetables 2 * Dairy 1 * Healthy fats and oils **3.5**

Smoky tempeh kale caesar

SERVES: 4 **PREP:** 20 MINS **COOK:** 20 MINS

17 g
TOTAL
FIBRE

★★★
FIBRE
RATING

√
RESISTANT
STARCH

4 thin slices wholemeal bread, torn into 1 cm cubes

1 bunch curly kale, stems removed, leaves roughly chopped

150 g brussels sprouts, trimmed and shredded

juice of ½ lemon

1 cos lettuce, cut into thin wedges

1 Lebanese cucumber, halved lengthways, thinly sliced into half moons

250 g cherry tomatoes, halved

2 tablespoons unsalted roasted almonds, roughly chopped

Smoky tempeh

340 g tempeh, sliced into thin strips

1 tablespoon smoked paprika

1 tablespoon extra virgin olive oil

Dressing

60 g parmesan, finely grated

½ small garlic clove, minced

juice of ½ lemon

⅓ cup (90 g) reduced-fat Greek-style yoghurt

1. Preheat the oven to 180°C (160°C fan-forced).
2. Spread out the bread cubes on a baking tray and bake for 10 minutes until crisp. Remove and set aside.
3. To prepare the smoky tempeh, place the tempeh, paprika and a small drizzle of olive oil in a bowl and toss to coat well. Heat half the remaining olive oil in a large frying pan over medium–high heat, add half the tempeh slices and cook for 3 minutes each side until golden brown and crisp. Remove and set aside. Repeat with the remaining olive oil and tempeh.
4. To make the dressing, mix together all the ingredients in a small bowl. Add 2 tablespoons water to thin it out (this helps it spread further over the salad).
5. Place the brussels sprouts and kale in a large bowl, drizzle over the lemon juice and use your hands to massage it into the greens for about 30 seconds until they soften. Add the lettuce, cucumber, cherry tomatoes and croutons and toss to combine. Pour over the dressing and lightly toss to coat well.
6. Divide the salad among four bowls, top with the tempeh and roasted almonds and serve.

Wholegrain high-fibre breads, cereals and legumes **1** ✳ Lean meat, fish, poultry, eggs, tofu and legumes **0.5** ✳ Fruit **0** ✳ Vegetables **2** ✳ Dairy **<0.5** ✳ Healthy fats and oils **2.5**

SERVES: 4   PREP: 35 MINS   COOK: 10 MINS

Tofu nori rolls

TOTAL FIBRE 13g

FIBRE RATING ★★★

RESISTANT STARCH √

2 teaspoons extra virgin olive oil

500 g firm tofu, cut into 1 cm thick batons

12 sheets nori

1 cup (140 g) Kimchi (see page 60)

3 cups coriander leaves, roughly chopped

2 Lebanese cucumbers, cut into 5 mm thick batons

1 carrot, shredded

1 bunch radishes, bulbs thinly sliced

2 cups (150 g) shredded cabbage

2 cups (370 g) cooked white rice (see pages 118–119)

2 tablespoons whole-egg mayonnaise

1 tablespoon sesame oil

1 tablespoon sesame seeds (white or black)

1. Heat the olive oil in a large non-stick frying pan over medium–high heat. Add the tofu (in batches if necessary) and cook for 2–3 minutes on each of the four sides until golden brown and crisp. Remove and set aside.

2. Set up your rolling station, with the nori, fried tofu, kimchi, coriander, prepared vegetables and a small bowl of water.

3. Combine the cooked rice, mayonnaise, sesame oil and sesame seeds in a bowl.

4. Place one nori sheet on your work surface, shiny side down, add 2 heaped tablespoons of the sesame rice and flatten out evenly, leaving a 3 cm strip at the top and bottom. Add an assortment of vegetables, coriander, kimchi and tofu in the lower half, then, starting at the bottom, roll up to form a log. Dip your fingers into the water and dampen the nori edge, then press to seal. Set aside and repeat with the remaining ingredients to make twelve rolls in total.

5. Slice the nori rolls in half and serve six small rolls per person. Any leftovers will keep in an airtight container in the fridge for up to 5 days.

Wholegrain high-fibre breads, cereals and legumes 1 ✳ Lean meat, fish, poultry, eggs, tofu and legumes 1 ✳ Fruit 0 ✳ Vegetables 2 ✳ Dairy 0 ✳ Healthy fats and oils 3

Herby green frittata

3g
TOTAL FIBRE

★
FIBRE RATING

1 tablespoon extra virgin olive oil

2 leeks, white part only, thinly sliced

2 garlic cloves, minced

5 Sicilian olives, pitted and roughly chopped

4 cups (160 g) silverbeet leaves, finely shredded

8 large free-range eggs, whisked

2 zucchini, grated, excess moisture squeezed out

3 tablespoons finely chopped dill

1 cup flat-leaf parsley leaves, roughly chopped

1 bunch chives, finely chopped

80 g reduced-fat cheddar, grated

80 g wholemeal plain flour

2 tablespoons pumpkin seeds (pepitas)

Butter lettuce salad

6 cups (150 g) butter lettuce leaves, roughly torn

1 bunch mint, leaves picked

½ medium avocado, sliced

juice of ½ lemon

2 teaspoons extra virgin olive oil

1. Preheat the oven to 180°C (160°C fan-forced) and line a 40 cm x 26 cm baking dish with baking paper.
2. Heat the olive oil in a large frying pan over medium heat. Add the leek, garlic and olives and cook, stirring, for 5 minutes or until softened. Add the silverbeet and cook for another 2 minutes until wilted. Transfer to a bowl and stir in the egg, zucchini, dill, parsley, chives and cheddar. Sprinkle over the flour and a generous pinch of freshly ground black pepper and stir again to combine.
3. Scoop the mixture into the prepared dish and smooth the surface. Sprinkle the pumpkin seeds over the top. Bake for 30 minutes, or until cooked through and the top is golden brown. Remove and set aside for a few minutes to cool while you make the salad.
4. For the salad, place the butter lettuce, mint and avocado in a large bowl. Squeeze over the lemon juice, drizzle with the olive oil and gently toss to coat.
5. Cut the frittata into four even pieces and serve with the butter lettuce salad.

TIP

For a gluten-free option, replace the wholemeal flour with buckwheat flour.

Wholegrain high-fibre breads, cereals and legumes **1** ✳ Lean meat, fish, poultry, eggs, tofu and legumes **1** ✳ Fruit **0** ✳ Vegetables **2** ✳ Dairy **0.5** ✳ Healthy fats and oils **3**

SERVES: 4   PREP: 25 MINS   COOK: 25 MINS

Pea falafels with brussels sprout slaw

23g
TOTAL FIBRE

★★★
FIBRE RATING

✓
RESISTANT STARCH

300 g cooked chickpeas (see pages 120–121)

2 cups (310 g) frozen peas

½ cup flat-leaf parsley leaves, roughly chopped

1 cup (150 g) quinoa flakes

1 large free-range egg

100 g reduced-fat fresh ricotta

1 garlic clove, minced

juice of ½ lemon

¼ teaspoon freshly ground black pepper

2 teaspoons extra virgin olive oil

Brussels sprout slaw

juice of 1 lemon

2 teaspoons Dijon mustard

2 teaspoons extra virgin olive oil

2 teaspoons whole-egg mayonnaise

2 tablespoons pumpkin seeds (pepitas)

300 g brussels sprouts, trimmed and shredded

4 cups (300 g) shredded green cabbage

1 baby fennel bulb, trimmed and thinly sliced

½ cup flat-leaf parsley leaves, roughly chopped

Tahini yoghurt

1½ tablespoons unhulled tahini

1 cup (250 g) reduced-fat Greek-style yoghurt

juice of ½ lemon

1. To make the brussels slaw, whisk together the lemon juice, mustard, olive oil, mayonnaise and 1 tablespoon water in a large bowl. Add the remaining ingredients and toss, using your hands to 'crunch' the slaw to help it soften and break down. Set aside to marinate while you make the falafels.

2. Place the chickpeas, peas, parsley, quinoa, egg, ricotta, garlic, lemon juice and pepper in a food processor and blitz to a chunky mixture.

3. Drizzle a little olive oil into a large non-stick frying pan and heat over medium heat. Working in batches of about six, form heaped tablespoons of the falafel mixture into rough balls (the mixture is sticky, so your hands will get a bit messy!). Place in the hot pan and push down slightly with a spatula. Cook for 3–4 minutes each side until golden brown and cooked through. Remove and set aside, then repeat with the remaining olive oil and falafel mix. You should have enough to make 16 falafels.

4. To make the tahini yoghurt, mix together all the ingredients and 2 tablespoons water in a bowl. If needed, add a little more water to reach a drizzle consistency.

5. Divide the falafels, slaw and tahini yoghurt among four plates and serve.

TIP

If you don't have cooked chickpeas prepared, you can use 1½ x 400 g tins of chickpeas instead. Choose salt-reduced options.

Wholegrain high-fibre breads, cereals and legumes **1** ✳ Lean meat, fish, poultry, eggs, tofu and legumes **0.5** ✳ Fruit **0** ✳ Vegetables **2** ✳ Dairy **0.5** ✳ Healthy fats and oils **4**

DINNER

Salmon with parsnip hash browns

9g

TOTAL
FIBRE

★★★

FIBRE
RATING

4 x 200 g boneless salmon fillets, skin on

grated lemon zest (optional)

1 lemon, sliced into wedges

Radish and cucumber salad

1 Lebanese cucumber, thinly sliced into discs

1 bunch radishes, bulbs thinly sliced

1½ cups (135 g) sugar snap peas, trimmed and cut into small chunks

3 tablespoons finely chopped dill

2 tablespoons reduced-fat Greek-style yoghurt

1 teaspoon poppy seeds

Parsnip hash browns

400 g parsnips, peeled

150 g potatoes, peeled

1 onion

2 free-range eggs

40 g wholemeal plain flour

⅓ cup (80 ml) extra virgin olive oil

1. To make the salad, place all the ingredients in a bowl and toss to combine. Set aside, allowing the yoghurt to soften the vegetables.

2. To make the hash browns, coarsely grate the parsnips, potato and onion (or push through the grater attachment of your food processor). Squeeze out as much moisture as possible – the more you squeeze out, the crisper your hash browns will be. Place in a large bowl with the eggs and flour and mix well to combine.

3. Heat a good drizzle of olive oil in a large non-stick frying pan over medium–high heat. Working in batches of two or three, add ½ cup of the mixture for each hash brown to the pan and flatten out to 1 cm thick fritters. Cook for 3–4 minutes each side, pushing down with a spatula to compact the mixture, until cooked through and a deep golden colour. Remove and drain on a plate lined with paper towel. Repeat with the remaining olive oil and mixture to make eight hash browns in total.

4. Return the frying pan including any remaining olive oil to medium–high heat and add the salmon fillets, skin side up. Cook for 4 minutes until golden brown, then flip and cook until the flesh feels firm to the touch and the skin is crispy, about 5 minutes.

5. Divide the salmon, hash browns and salad evenly among four plates. Finish with a generous grinding of black pepper and lemon zest, if you like, and serve with lemon wedges.

Wholegrain high-fibre breads, cereals and legumes 1 ✳ Lean meat, fish, poultry, eggs, tofu and legumes 2 ✳ Fruit 0 ✳ Vegetables 2 ✳ Dairy 0 ✳ Healthy fats and oils 4

SERVES: 4   PREP: 20 MINS   COOK: 40 MINS

Cauliflower fish cakes with watercress salad

15g
TOTAL
FIBRE

★★★
FIBRE
RATING

√
RESISTANT
STARCH

2 cups (200 g) roughly chopped cauliflower florets

550 g skinless, boneless white fish fillets (such as snapper or barramundi), cut into large chunks

2 garlic cloves, crushed

3 tablespoons finely chopped dill

250 g cooked cannellini beans (see pages 120–121) or drained and rinsed tinned cannellini beans

⅓ cup (50 g) quinoa flakes

2 free-range eggs

finely grated zest of ½ lemon

¼ teaspoon freshly ground black pepper

1 tablespoon extra virgin olive oil

lemon wedges, to serve

Watercress salad

1 tablespoon extra virgin olive oil

2 teaspoons Dijon mustard

juice of ½ lemon

4 cups (120 g) watercress sprigs

150 g sugar snap peas, trimmed and halved

1 baby fennel bulb, trimmed and very thinly sliced

1 cup (155 g) frozen peas, thawed

1 small zucchini, very thinly sliced

½ medium avocado, sliced

50 g reduced-fat goat's feta

2 tablespoons unsalted roasted almonds, roughly chopped

1. Place the cauliflower in a saucepan, cover with water and place over high heat. Bring to a gentle boil and cook for 8 minutes or until tender.
2. Place the fish pieces in a food processor and blitz a few times to break them into smaller chunks. Add the cooked cauliflower and remaining ingredients (except the olive oil) and blitz to combine. You can make the cakes completely smooth or leave small chunks of fish and cauliflower for texture – it's up to you. Form the mixture into eight or 12 even balls.
3. Heat a drizzle of olive oil in a large frying pan over medium–high heat. Add four balls and gently push down to flatten into patties. Cook for 4–5 minutes each side until golden brown and cooked through. Remove to a plate and cover to keep warm. Repeat with the remaining olive oil and fish cakes.
4. To make the watercress salad, whisk together the olive oil, lemon, mustard and about 2 teaspoons water in a large bowl. Add the remaining ingredients and toss to coat the salad in the dressing.
5. Divide the cauliflower fish cakes among four plates and serve with the watercress salad and lemon wedges for squeezing.

Wholegrain high-fibre breads, cereals and legumes **0.5** ✳ Lean meat, fish, poultry, eggs, tofu and legumes **2** ✳ Fruit **0** ✳ Vegetables **2** ✳ Dairy **0.5** ✳ Healthy fats and oils **4**

Tofu gado gado bowl

21g
TOTAL
FIBRE

★★★
FIBRE
RATING

√
RESISTANT
STARCH

2 teaspoons extra virgin olive oil

1.36 kg firm tofu, cut into 1 cm thick triangles

1 tablespoon curry powder

2 cups (370 g) cooked white rice (see pages 118–119)

1 large carrot, grated

2 Lebanese cucumbers, halved lengthways and thinly sliced into half moons

2 cups (150 g) shredded purple cabbage

1 bunch radishes, bulbs thinly sliced

4 cups shredded (200 g) cos or iceberg lettuce

1 cup coriander leaves

Peanut sauce

2½ tablespoons crunchy peanut butter (no added sugar or salt)

juice of 1 lime

2 teaspoons sesame oil

1 small garlic clove, minced

1 cm piece ginger, peeled and minced

1. To make the peanut sauce, place all the ingredients and 2 tablespoons tepid water in a bowl and mix together well. Add a little more water if needed to thin it out to a drizzle consistency. If your peanut butter is really sticky, keep at it – you'll create a nice smooth dressing with some good stirring. Set aside for serving.

2. Heat half the olive oil in a large frying pan over medium–high heat. Add half the tofu pieces and sprinkle over half the curry powder, then cook for 2–3 minutes each side until golden brown. Repeat with the remaining olive oil, tofu and curry powder.

3. Divide the cooked rice, fried tofu, carrot, cucumber, cabbage, radish, lettuce and coriander among four bowls and top with a good spoonful of peanut sauce. Toss together and serve.

TIP

This recipe provides four large portions of tofu, so depending on your appetite you may not eat it all! Leftovers can be refrigerated and are delicious for lunch the next day.

Wholegrain high-fibre breads, cereals and legumes 1 ✳ Lean meat, fish, poultry, eggs, tofu and legumes 2 ✳ Fruit **0** ✳ Vegetables **2.5** ✳ Dairy **0** ✳ Healthy fats and oils **4**

SERVES: 4 **PREP:** 20 MINS **COOK:** 1 HOUR 15 MINS

Braised artichoke with sage, lemon and fennel

41g
TOTAL FIBRE

★★★
FIBRE RATING

√
RESISTANT STARCH

6 (800 g) whole artichokes

3 tablespoons extra virgin olive oil

2 golden shallots, thinly sliced

1 fennel bulb, trimmed and cut into 4 cm chunks

2 zucchini, halved lengthways and sliced into 1 cm thick half moons

8 green olives, pitted and torn in half

pinch of dried chilli flakes

5 garlic cloves, crushed

4 sprigs sage, leaves picked and roughly chopped

1 tablespoon apple cider vinegar

1 cup (250 ml) salt-reduced vegetable stock

1.2 kg cooked cannellini beans (see pages 120–121) or drained and rinsed tinned cannellini beans

juice of 1 lemon

½ cup flat-leaf parsley leaves, roughly chopped

4 thin slices sourdough bread, toasted

1. Preheat the oven to 180°C (160°C fan-forced).
2. Start by prepping the artichokes. Working with one at a time, remove all the outer leaves, and slice off the top quarter of the artichoke. Cut it in half and scoop out the hairy 'choke' with a spoon. Using a vegetable peeler, peel the stem until you are left with the fleshy interior.
3. Heat a large deep frying pan over medium–high heat. Add half the olive oil and the shallot and cook for 2 minutes or until softened. Add the remaining oil, then the artichoke, fennel, zucchini, olives, chilli flakes, garlic and sage and cook for a further 2–3 minutes, or until everything is well incorporated and the garlic is fragrant.
4. Deglaze the pan with the vinegar, and cook for another 1 minute.
5. Divide the vegetables between two large baking dishes and add half the stock to each. Cover with foil and place in the oven for 60–70 minutes until the artichoke and fennel are tender.
6. Remove the dishes from the oven. Stir through the beans, then squeeze over the lemon juice and top with the parsley. Scoop into four bowls and serve with sourdough toast.

TIP

This recipe makes four large portions containing plenty of gut-friendly beans. Leftovers can be frozen for an easy weeknight meal.

Wholegrain high-fibre breads, cereals and legumes **1** ✳ Lean meat, fish, poultry, eggs, tofu and legumes **2** ✳ Fruit **0** ✳ Vegetables **2** ✳ Dairy **0** ✳ Healthy fats and oils **3.5**

Golden fish tacos with the lot

14g

TOTAL
FIBRE

★★★

FIBRE
RATING

2 teaspoons extra virgin olive oil

4 corn cobs, husk and silks removed, kernels sliced off (see tip)

1½ teaspoons smoked paprika

4 small corn tortillas

300 g cherry tomatoes, quartered

2 Lebanese cucumbers, halved lengthways, seeds scooped out, thinly sliced into half moons

1 bunch radishes, bulbs halved

1 head butter lettuce, leaves torn

lime wedges, to serve

Avocado whip

1 small avocado (155 g flesh)

3 tablespoons reduced-fat Greek-style yoghurt

juice of 1 lime

Golden fish

3 teaspoons extra virgin olive oil

800 g skinless, boneless white fish fillets (such as snapper or barramundi)

2 teaspoons ground turmeric

1. To make the avocado whip, scoop the avocado flesh into a bowl and mash with a fork. Add the yoghurt and lime and season with a pinch of freshly ground black pepper. Mix to combine and set aside.

2. Heat the olive oil in a large frying pan over medium–high heat, add the corn kernels and paprika and cook, tossing regularly, for 4–5 minutes until softened. Tip into a bowl and cover with foil to keep warm for serving.

3. Return the frying pan to medium–high heat. Add the tortillas in batches and cook for 1 minute each side until warmed through. Stack onto a plate and cover with foil to keep warm.

4. To prepare the golden fish, place the pan back over medium–high heat and add the olive oil. Once hot, add the fish fillets in batches, sprinkle with turmeric and freshly ground black pepper and cook for 4 minutes each side until just cooked through. Transfer to a serving plate and flake with a fork.

5. Take the flaked fish, avocado whip, paprika corn, tortillas, tomato, cucumber, radish and butter lettuce to the table. Let everyone fill their own tacos and serve the rest as a salad with lime wedges alongside.

> ## TIP
>
> To easily slice the kernels off a corn cob, remove the husks and silks, then lay the cob flat on a cutting board and cut down the side to remove the kernels. Rotate and continue cutting until all kernels have been removed.

Wholegrain high-fibre breads, cereals and legumes 1 ✳ Lean meat, fish, poultry, eggs, tofu and legumes 2 ✳ Fruit 0 ✳ Vegetables 2.5 ✳ Dairy 0 ✳ Healthy fats and oils 3

Mediterranean chickpea stew

31g
TOTAL
FIBRE

★★★
FIBRE
RATING

√
RESISTANT
STARCH

2 tablespoons extra virgin olive oil
2 onions, thinly sliced
3 sticks celery, diced
2 zucchini, finely diced
1 fennel bulb, trimmed and thinly sliced
3 garlic cloves, minced
10 sundried tomatoes, chopped
½ teaspoon dried chilli flakes
2 tablespoons apple cider vinegar
1 litre salt-reduced vegetable stock
1.2 kg cooked chickpeas (see pages 120–121) or drained and rinsed tinned chickpeas (choose salt-reduced options)
6 kale or cavolo nero leaves, stalks removed and roughly chopped
1 cup flat-leaf parsley leaves
juice of 1 lemon
80 g parmesan, shaved

1. Heat the olive oil in a large saucepan over medium heat, add the onion, celery and zucchini and cook for 7 minutes or until the onion has softened. Add the fennel, garlic, sundried tomato and chilli flakes and cook, stirring, for another 5 minutes, until the garlic is fragrant and the fennel is starting to soften. Add the vinegar and stir through until it has evaporated.
2. Pour in the stock, add the chickpeas and bring to a gentle boil, then reduce the heat and simmer for 10 minutes to allow the flavours to mingle. The stew is ready when the fennel is soft to the bite.
3. Remove from the heat and stir through the kale or cavolo nero, parsley and lemon juice until the kale or cavalo nero has wilted.
4. Spoon the stew into four bowls and top with shaved parmesan and a good grinding of black pepper.

TIPS

This recipe makes four large portions, with plenty of gut-friendly chickpeas. You can divide leftovers among airtight containers and freeze for up to 3 months, ready for another delicious dinner.

Wholegrain high-fibre breads, cereals and legumes **0** ✳ Lean meat, fish, poultry, eggs, tofu and legumes **2** ✳ Fruit **0** ✳ Vegetables **2.5** ✳ Dairy **0.5** ✳ Healthy fats and oils **2**

Okonomiyaki pancakes

11g
TOTAL
FIBRE

★★★
FIBRE
RATING

12 free-range eggs

½ savoy cabbage (800 g), shredded

1 zucchini, grated, excess moisture squeezed out

1 cup (100 g) wholemeal breadcrumbs

1 cup (65 g) sliced spring onion

340 g firm tofu

2 teaspoons extra virgin olive oil

To serve

3 tablespoons Kewpie mayonnaise

3 tablespoons sriracha chilli sauce (optional)

1 sheet nori, sliced into thin strips

2 teaspoons sesame seeds

4 cups (80 g) mixed salad leaves

1. Crack the eggs into a large bowl and lightly beat with a whisk. Add the cabbage, zucchini, breadcrumbs and most of the spring onion and mix really well to combine. Put the tofu in a food processor and blitz until it resembles rice, then fold the tofu through the okonomiyaki mixture.

2. Heat ½ teaspoon olive oil in a large non-stick frying pan. Add one-quarter of the okonomiyaki mixture and push down with a spatula. Cook for 6–7 minutes, until the bottom is golden brown, then carefully flip the pancake over. An easy way to do this is to place a large plate over the frying pan and flip the pancake onto the plate, then slide it back into the pan. Cook for another 5 minutes until the egg is set and the pancake is golden brown.

3. Remove to a plate and cover to keep warm. Repeat with the remaining olive oil and okonomiyaki mixture. To speed things up, cook two pancakes at once if you have two large frying pans.

4. Decorate the pancakes with lines of mayonnaise and sriracha chilli sauce (if using), top with nori, sesame seeds and mixed salad leaves, and serve.

> ### TIP
>
> If you want to create thin lines with your mayonnaise drizzle, place the mayonnaise in a ziplock bag and snip a little bit off one corner. Use as you would a piping bag.

Wholegrain high-fibre breads, cereals and legumes **1** ✳ Lean meat, fish, poultry, eggs, tofu and legumes **2** ✳ Fruit **0** ✳ Vegetables **2** ✳ Dairy **0** ✳ Healthy fats and oils **3.5**

Green seed bowl

32g TOTAL FIBRE

★★★ FIBRE RATING

√ RESISTANT STARCH

8 large free-range eggs

2 heads broccoli, cut into small florets

2 cups (200 g) frozen edamame (or frozen peas)

2 tablespoons pumpkin seeds (pepitas)

1 tablespoon sunflower seeds

1 tablespoon flaxseeds

3 cups (360 g) cooked white quinoa (see pages 118–119)

600 g cooked cannellini beans (see pages 120–121) or drained and rinsed tinned cannellini beans

1 baby cos lettuce, chopped

4 cups (60 g) cavolo nero

1 zucchini, shredded

Golden tahini dressing

2 tablespoons unhulled tahini

2 teaspoons extra virgin olive oil

¼ teaspoon ground turmeric

juice of ½ lemon

1. Half-fill a large saucepan with water and bring to the boil over medium–high heat. Add the eggs and cook for exactly 7 minutes, then remove with a slotted spoon and plunge into cold water to stop them cooking. When cool enough to handle, peel the eggs and cut them in half lengthways.

2. Add the broccoli and edamame to the boiling water and cook for 2 minutes. Drain, then refresh under cold water.

3. Meanwhile, to make the golden tahini dressing, mix together all the ingredients in a small bowl. Stir in 2–4 tablespoons warm water to thin the dressing to your preferred consistency (don't use cold water as it will make the tahini seize up).

4. Heat a large frying pan over medium heat and toast the pumpkin seeds, sunflower seeds and flaxseeds, tossing, for 3–4 minutes until nicely golden.

5. Place the cooked quinoa, cannellini beans, broccoli, edamame, cos lettuce, cavolo nero and zucchini in a large bowl and gently toss together.

6. Divide the salad among four bowls, top with the egg halves and sprinkle over the toasted seeds. Drizzle over the dressing and serve.

Wholegrain high-fibre breads, cereals and legumes 1 ✳ Lean meat, fish, poultry, eggs, tofu and legumes 2 ✳ Fruit 0 ✳ Vegetables 2 ✳ Dairy 0 ✳ Healthy fats and oils 4

Wholesome roast chicken dinner

12 g
TOTAL FIBRE

★★★
FIBRE RATING

✓
RESISTANT STARCH

1 bunch tarragon, leaves picked and finely chopped

3 garlic cloves, finely minced

1 tablespoon white vinegar

2 tablespoons extra virgin olive oil

1 x 1.5 kg chicken

600 g sweet potatoes, cut into 3 cm chunks

3 red onions, cut into wedges

Radicchio salad

3 tablespoons walnuts

2 teaspoons Dijon mustard

juice of 1 lemon

1 tablespoon extra virgin olive oil

1 head radicchio, leaves roughly torn

1 bunch radishes, bulbs thinly sliced

1 fennel bulb, trimmed and thinly sliced

1 blood orange (or regular orange), peeled and sliced

1. Preheat the oven to 200°C (180°C fan-forced).
2. In a small bowl, mix together the tarragon, garlic, vinegar, 1 tablespoon olive oil and a good pinch of freshly ground black pepper.
3. Place the chicken in a roasting tin, then massage the tarragon mixture into the chicken, making sure it is well coated. Roast for 1 hour 10 minutes, until the juices run clear when the thickest part of the thigh is pierced with a skewer. Remove from the oven, cover with foil and rest for 10 minutes before carving.
4. Meanwhile, place the sweet potato and onion on a large baking tray and drizzle over the remaining olive oil. Place in the oven and roast for 45–55 minutes, until the veggies are well and truly caramelised.
5. To prepare the radicchio salad, crumble the walnuts into a frying pan over medium heat and cook, tossing regularly, for 3–4 minutes, until toasted and lightly golden. Set aside.
6. Whisk together the mustard, lemon juice, olive oil and 1 tablespoon water in a large bowl. Add the remaining ingredients, including the toasted walnuts, and toss to coat well.
7. Remove the skin and visible fat from the chicken and carve into pieces. Divide among four plates and serve with the roasted veggies and radicchio salad.

Wholegrain high-fibre breads, cereals and legumes **1** ✳ Lean meat, fish, poultry, eggs, tofu and legumes **2**
✳ Fruit **<0.5** ✳ Vegetables **2** ✳ Dairy **0** ✳ Healthy fats and oils **3**

Curried chicken with golden crispy rice

16 g

TOTAL
FIBRE

★★★

FIBRE
RATING

800 g chicken thigh fillets, skin and visible fat removed

2 tablespoons curry powder

2 teaspoons ground cumin

1 tablespoon extra virgin olive oil

2 tablespoons raw almonds, roughly chopped

300 g sugar snap peas, ends trimmed

2 bunches broccolini, halved lengthways

2 cups mint leaves

2 cups flat-leaf parsley leaves

2 cups coriander leaves

juice of ½ lime

2 Lebanese cucumbers, sliced into thin discs

Golden crispy rice

¾ cup (150 g) basmati rice

¼ teaspoon ground turmeric

5 golden shallots, thinly sliced

2 tablespoons extra virgin olive oil

1. To make the golden crispy rice, place the rice and turmeric in a saucepan, add 1½ cups (375 ml) water and bring to the boil. Reduce the heat and simmer, covered, for 10 minutes. Remove and set aside, leaving the lid on for the rice to steam.
2. Meanwhile, place the chicken, curry powder and cumin in a large bowl and toss to coat the chicken evenly. Heat the olive oil in a large frying pan over medium–high heat, add the chicken and cook for 4–5 minutes each side until golden brown and cooked through. Remove to a plate and cover with foil to rest and keep warm.
3. To finish the golden crispy rice, add the shallot and olive oil to the same pan. Cook, stirring occasionally, for 5 minutes until softened and golden. Add the cooked rice and stir to combine, then press down on the rice with a spatula to flatten it. Cook for 6–7 minutes, without stirring, until a golden crust forms on the bottom. Using your spatula, flip big chunks of the rice over (it will break apart, but try and keep some sections stuck together), then push down into the pan for another 5 minutes until dark brown. Remove and set aside for serving.
4. Return the frying pan to medium–high heat. Add the almonds, sugar snap peas and broccolini and cook, tossing, for 3–5 minutes until the veggies are tender.
5. Mix together the mint, parsley, coriander and lime juice in a bowl.
6. Divide the curried chicken, crispy rice and cucumber evenly among bowls, top with the veggies and dressed herbs and serve.

Wholegrain high-fibre breads, cereals and legumes 1 ✳ Lean meat, fish, poultry, eggs, tofu and legumes 2 ✳ Fruit 0 ✳ Vegetables 2.5 ✳ Dairy 0 ✳ Healthy fats and oils 4

Chicken meatballs with peas and asparagus

10 g
TOTAL
FIBRE

FIBRE
RATING

RESISTANT
STARCH

2 bunches spring onions, thinly sliced

1 cup (155 g) frozen peas

1 teaspoon sumac

2 teaspoons capers, rinsed

finely grated zest and juice of ½ lemon

1 teaspoon Dijon mustard

2 tablespoons extra virgin olive oil

5 bunches asparagus, woody ends trimmed

3 zucchini, halved lengthways and sliced into 1 cm thick half moons

mint and flat-leaf parsley leaves, to serve

Chicken meatballs

800 g lean minced chicken

1 large free-range egg

½ cup (55 g) almond meal

½ cup finely chopped flat-leaf parsley

1. To make the chicken meatballs, place all the ingredients in a large bowl and mix with your hands until well combined. Cover and chill in the fridge for 15 minutes to allow the mixture to firm up.

2. Meanwhile, place the spring onions, peas, sumac, capers, lemon zest and juice and mustard in a saucepan, along with 3 tablespoons water and a pinch of freshly ground black pepper. Cook, stirring often, over medium–low heat for 2–3 minutes until the spring onion has wilted and the peas have thawed. Remove from the heat. (If you cook them for any longer the peas will start to turn grey, and you want them nice and green.)

3. Form the chicken mixture into golf ball-sized meatballs.

4. Heat the olive oil in a large non-stick frying pan over medium–high heat, add the meatballs and cook, turning regularly, for 4 minutes or until browned all over. Reduce the heat to medium, cover with a lid and cook for another 3–4 minutes, until the meatballs are cooked through. Remove and keep warm.

5. Add the asparagus and zucchini to the same pan (no need to clean it first), still over medium heat. Toss to coat in the residual oil, then add 2 tablespoons water and cover with a lid. Allow to steam for 1–2 minutes until just tender, regularly shaking the pan to move the veggies around.

6. Divide all the veggies and meatballs among four plates and serve scattered with the mint and parsley.

Wholegrain high-fibre breads, cereals and legumes **0** ✳ Lean meat, fish, poultry, eggs, tofu and legumes **2** ✳ Fruit **0** ✳ Vegetables **4** ✳ Dairy **0** ✳ Healthy fats and oils **4**

Chicken Traybakes

Valentine's chicken

SERVES: 4 **PREP:** 15 MINS **COOK:** 1 HOUR 10 MINS

13g
TOTAL
FIBRE

★★★
FIBRE
RATING

2 tablespoons extra virgin olive oil

4 large bone-in chicken marylands, skin and visible fat removed (see tip)

900 g truss cherry tomatoes on the vine, or regular cherry tomatoes

3 red capsicums, cut into 3 cm chunks

2 red onions, cut into 1 cm thick wedges

2 long red chillies, seeded if you like, cut into 1 cm chunks

1½ teaspoons capers, rinsed

6 garlic cloves, minced

1 bunch basil, leaves picked

½ cup (125 ml) salt-reduced chicken stock

4 thin slices sourdough bread, toasted

1. Preheat the oven to 180°C (160°C fan-forced).
2. Heat 1 tablespoon olive oil in a large frying pan over high heat. Once the oil is hot, add two chicken marylands and cook for 2 minutes each side, or until browned. Set aside and repeat with the remaining marylands.
3. Place the cherry tomatoes, capsicum, onion, chilli, capers and garlic in a large baking dish (or two smaller dishes if you don't have one big enough). Add most of the basil leaves, reserving a small handful for garnish. Drizzle over the remaining olive oil and toss to coat well, then nestle in the chicken marylands. Pour over the chicken stock and any chicken pan juices. Place in the oven and bake for 1 hour, or until the chicken is cooked through and the veggies are very tender and starting to collapse.
4. Take the dish out of the oven, transfer the chicken to a plate and remove the skin. Using a potato masher or fork, lightly crush the vegetables.
5. Divide the chicken and vegetables among four plates and season with a pinch of freshly ground black pepper. Garnish with the reserved basil and serve with the sourdough toast.

TIP

If you can't find chicken marylands, use a butterflied chicken instead. It will cook in the same amount of time.

Wholegrain high-fibre breads, cereals and legumes **1** ✳ Lean meat, fish, poultry, eggs, tofu and legumes **2** ✳ Fruit **0** ✳ Vegetables **3** ✳ Dairy **0** ✳ Healthy fats and oils **2**

**Sumac chicken with
tahini yoghurt**
PAGE 182

Greek oregano chicken
traybake
PAGE 183

Sumac chicken with tahini yoghurt

TOTAL FIBRE | FIBRE RATING | RESISTANT STARCH

SERVES: 4 **PREP:** 20 MINS **COOK:** 55 MINS

1 head cauliflower, cut into florets
2 eggplants, cut into 4 cm chunks
1 large sweet potato, cut into 4 cm chunks
2 red onions, cut into wedges
1½ tablespoons ground cumin
4 garlic cloves, crushed
2 tablespoons olive oil
1 tablespoon pine nuts
½ cup flat-leaf parsley leaves

Sumac chicken

800 g chicken breast fillets
2 tablespoons sumac
1 tablespoon ground cinnamon
1 tablespoon ground cumin
juice of ½ lemon
1 teaspoon extra virgin olive oil

Tahini yoghurt

1 cup (250 g) reduced-fat Greek-style yoghurt
1 tablespoon unhulled tahini
finely grated zest and juice of ½ lemon

1. Preheat the oven to 180°C (160°C fan-forced).
2. Spread the cauliflower, eggplant, sweet potato and red onion across two large baking trays. Sprinkle evenly with the cumin and crushed garlic and drizzle over the olive oil. Toss to coat well, then place in the oven and roast for 30–40 minutes until the veggies are tender.
3. Meanwhile, to prepare the sumac chicken, place the chicken in a large bowl, add the spices, lemon juice and a good pinch of freshly ground black pepper and massage into the chicken. Heat the olive oil in a large frying pan over high heat, add the chicken and sear for 1–2 minutes each side until well browned all over. (You may need to work in batches.)
4. Remove the trays from the oven and nestle the seared chicken among the veggies. Sprinkle the pine nuts over the top. Return to the oven and roast for another 12–15 minutes, until the chicken is cooked through and the pine nuts are golden. Slice the chicken.
5. To make the tahini yoghurt, mix together all the ingredients in a small bowl. Add 1–2 tablespoons tepid water and mix to a drizzling consistency.
6. Divide the sumac chicken, roasted veggies and pine nuts among four plates. Drizzle the tahini yoghurt over the top, scatter over the parsley leaves and serve.

Wholegrain high-fibre breads, cereals and legumes 1 ✳ Lean meat, fish, poultry, eggs, tofu and legumes 2 ✳ Fruit 0 ✳ Vegetables 3 ✳ Dairy <0.5 ✳ Healthy fats and oils 4

Greek oregano chicken traybake

13g

TOTAL FIBRE **FIBRE RATING** **RESISTANT STARCH**

SERVES: 4 **PREP:** 20 MINS **COOK:** 1 HOUR

1.2 kg bone-in chicken pieces (thighs, breast or drumsticks), skin removed (800 g chicken meat)

3 tablespoons oregano leaves, finely chopped

finely grated zest and juice of ½ lemon

1½ tablespoons extra virgin olive oil

600 g potato, peeled and cut into 3 cm chunks

2 onions, thickly sliced

4 garlic cloves, skin on

300 g green beans, trimmed

2 zucchini, sliced into 2 cm thick rounds

3 tomatoes, cut into wedges

80 g reduced-fat feta, crumbled

2 tablespoons unsalted roasted almonds, roughly chopped

Oregano sauce

½ cup oregano leaves

2 cups flat-leaf parsley leaves

juice of 1 lemon

10 green olives, pitted

1 tablespoon apple cider vinegar

1 tablespoon extra virgin olive oil

pinch of dried chilli flakes

1. Preheat the oven to 200°C (180°C fan-forced).
2. Place the chicken in a large bowl, sprinkle over the oregano, lemon zest and juice and season with a good grinding of black pepper. Toss to coat well.
3. Heat 2 teaspoons olive oil in a large frying pan over high heat, add the chicken and sear for 3 minutes each side until golden brown.
4. Divide the chicken, potato and onion between two large baking trays and spread out in a single layer. Drizzle 1 teaspoon olive oil over each tray and scatter the garlic cloves over the top. Bake for 30 minutes.
5. Meanwhile, place the green beans and zucchini in a large bowl and toss with the remaining olive oil.
6. Remove the trays from the oven, remove the garlic cloves and set aside. Scatter over the zucchini and green beans, then bake for another 20 minutes or until the greens are wilted and cooked through.
7. Meanwhile, to make the oregano sauce, squeeze the flesh from the garlic cloves into a food processor. Add the sauce ingredients and pulse to a chunky paste.
8. Divide the baked chicken and vegetables among four plates. Serve with the tomato, feta, almonds and oregano sauce.

TIP

For a good source of resistant starch, boil the potatoes and allow them to cool overnight, and bake as per the recipe.

Wholegrain high-fibre breads, cereals and legumes **1** ✳ Lean meat, fish, poultry, eggs, tofu and legumes **2** ✳ Fruit **0** ✳ Vegetables **2** ✳ Dairy **0.5** ✳ Healthy fats and oils **4**

Pork with celeriac and white bean puree

20 g TOTAL FIBRE   ★★★ FIBRE RATING   ✓ RESISTANT STARCH

2 tablespoons extra virgin olive oil

4 x 200 g pork loin chops, excess fat removed

2 large onions, thinly sliced

1 zucchini, thinly sliced

2 garlic cloves, minced

200 g brown mushrooms, sliced

4 sprigs thyme, leaves picked

1 tablespoon apple cider vinegar

2 tablespoons Dijon mustard

2 cups (500 ml) salt-reduced chicken stock

1 tablespoon tapioca flour

2 cups (60 g) watercress sprigs

Celeriac and white bean puree

2 small or 1 large celeriac (600 g), peeled and cut into 2–3 cm chunks

1½ cups (240 g) cooked cannellini beans (see pages 120–121) or drained and rinsed tinned cannellini beans

3 tablespoons salt-reduced chicken stock, plus extra if needed

¼ teaspoon freshly ground black pepper

1. To make the celeriac and white bean puree, place the celeriac in a large saucepan and pour in enough water to cover by 3 cm. Place over high heat and bring to the boil, then reduce the heat to medium–low and simmer for 13–15 minutes, until the celeriac is tender. Drain, then return the celeriac to the pan and add the remaining ingredients. Using a stick blender, blitz to a smooth puree, adding a little more stock if needed. (Alternatively, transfer everything to an upright blender and pulse until smooth.) Cover with a lid to keep warm and set aside.

2. Meanwhile, heat the olive oil in a large frying pan over medium–high heat. Once hot, add the pork chops, in batches if necessary, and cook for 4 minutes each side until golden brown. Remove to a plate, cover with foil and leave to rest.

3. Add the onion and zucchini to the pan and cook, stirring occasionally, for 5–6 minutes until softened. Add the garlic, mushroom and thyme and cook, stirring, for another 3–5 minutes, until the mushroom has softened. Pour in the apple cider vinegar and stir to deglaze the pan, then add the mustard and stir through. Add the stock and mix to combine, then add the tapioca flour and whisk into the liquid until the sauce thickens. Return the pork chops to the pan and turn to coat in the sauce.

4. Divide the celeriac and white bean puree among four shallow bowls or plates and top with a pork chop. Spoon over the onion and mushroom sauce, season with a good grinding of black pepper and serve with sprigs of watercress.

Wholegrain high-fibre breads, cereals and legumes **1** ✳ Lean meat, fish, poultry, eggs, tofu and legumes **2** ✳ Fruit **0** ✳ Vegetables **2** ✳ Dairy **0** ✳ Healthy fats and oils **2**

TIPS

✳ To prepare a celeriac, place it on a
chopping board and use a knife to remove
the top and base so it sits flat. Peel by
slicing carefully down the sides, trying not
to remove too much of the white flesh
underneath. Chop or slice as desired.

✳ If you can't find celeriac, use 600 g
parsnip instead.

Lemongrass steak skewers with tabbouleh

 11g
TOTAL FIBRE

 ★★★
FIBRE RATING

 √
RESISTANT STARCH

2 stalks lemongrass, base and tough outer leaves removed, roughly chopped

¼–½ teaspoon dried chilli flakes

5 cm piece ginger, peeled and roughly chopped

4 garlic cloves, roughly chopped

⅓ cup (80 ml) rice wine vinegar

¼ teaspoon freshly ground black pepper

800 g rump or flank steak, visible fat removed, sliced into long 2 cm thick strips

1 tablespoon extra virgin olive oil

3 green capsicums, thickly sliced

lemon wedges, to serve

Tabbouleh

3 cups (360 g) cooked white quinoa (see pages 118–119)

1 small red onion, finely diced

1 Lebanese cucumber, finely diced

250 g cherry tomatoes (or 2 small regular tomatoes), chopped

1 cup mint leaves, finely chopped

1 cup flat-leaf parsley leaves, finely chopped

1 cup coriander leaves, finely chopped

3 tablespoons unsalted pistachio kernels, finely chopped

2 tablespoons pumpkin seeds (pepitas)

1 tablespoon extra virgin olive oil

juice of 1 lemon

1. Place the lemongrass, chilli flakes, ginger, garlic, rice wine vinegar and pepper in a food processor or blender and blitz to form a chunky paste. Tip into a large shallow bowl, add the steak strips and turn to coat. Thread the steak evenly onto 12 skewers (use metal skewers if you have them; if not, soak wooden skewers in water for a few minutes before threading so they don't burn).

2. Preheat a barbecue grill or flat plate to high. Brush the skewers with olive oil, then place on the hot plate with the capsicum and cook for 1–2 minutes each side until lightly charred on the outside. If you don't have a barbecue, heat a large frying pan or chargrill pan over high heat, then drizzle the olive oil into the pan instead of brushing the skewers. Cook as above. Remove the skewers and set aside to rest for a few minutes.

3. To make the tabbouleh, combine all the ingredients in a bowl.

4. Divide the tabbouleh and skewers among four plates and serve with lemon wedges.

Wholegrain high-fibre breads, cereals and legumes 1 ✳ Lean meat, fish, poultry, eggs, tofu and legumes 2 ✳ Fruit 0 ✳ Vegetables 2 ✳ Dairy 0 ✳ Healthy fats and oils 4

Warming pork congee

7g
TOTAL
FIBRE

★★★
FIBRE
RATING

✓
RESISTANT
STARCH

1 tablespoon extra-virgin olive oil

800 g lean minced pork

2 teaspoons sesame oil

250 g mushrooms, thinly sliced

1 large zucchini, diced

4 garlic cloves, minced

3 cm piece ginger, peeled and minced

1 bunch spring onions, finely chopped

1 bunch bok choy, roughly chopped

½ small head cauliflower

¾ cup (150 g) jasmine rice

1 litre salt-reduced chicken stock

2 cups coriander leaves

¼ teaspoon dried chilli flakes

2 teaspoons black sesame seeds

2 tablespoons unsalted roasted peanuts

1. Heat the olive oil in a large saucepan over medium–high heat. Add the pork mince and cook for 7–8 minutes until browned, stirring and breaking up any large lumps as you go. Add the sesame oil, mushroom and zucchini and cook for 2 minutes until slightly softened. Add the garlic, ginger, spring onion and bok choy and cook for 1–2 minutes, until the vegetables are softened and the garlic is fragrant. Transfer to a bowl, cover and set aside.

2. Grate the cauliflower, either with a box grater or put it through a food processor with a grater attachment. You should have 3 cups of cauliflower 'rice'.

3. Add the cauliflower, jasmine rice, stock and 3 cups (750 ml) water to the pan and scrape up any of the browned bits caught on the bottom. Bring to the boil, then reduce the heat to low and simmer for 40–50 minutes, stirring every 10 minutes, until the congee reaches a porridge consistency. Add a little more water if you prefer it a bit thinner.

4. While still over the heat, stir through half the reserved pork and vegetable mixture for 1–2 minutes until warmed through.

5. Divide the congee among four bowls and top with the remaining pork mixture. Sprinkle over the coriander, chilli flakes, sesame seeds and peanuts, and serve.

Wholegrain high-fibre breads, cereals and legumes **1** ✳ Lean meat, fish, poultry, eggs, tofu and legumes **2** ✳ Fruit **0** ✳ Vegetables **2.5** ✳ Dairy **0** ✳ Healthy fats and oils **2.5**

SERVES: 4   PREP: 20 MINS   COOK: 30 MINS

Sesame beef with Korean corn cheese

11g TOTAL FIBRE   ★★★ FIBRE RATING

2 garlic cloves, minced

2 teaspoons sesame oil

2 teaspoons apple cider vinegar

800 g flank beef steaks, excess fat removed

1 tablespoon extra virgin olive oil

600 g green beans, trimmed

Korean corn cheese

1 tablespoon extra virgin olive oil

2 golden shallots, thinly sliced

4 corn cobs, husks and silks removed, kernels sliced off (see tip on page 164)

1 teaspoon cayenne pepper

4 spring onions, thinly sliced

60 g reduced-fat feta, crumbled

80 g mozzarella, grated

1. Combine the garlic, sesame oil and vinegar in a large bowl, add the beef steaks and toss well to coat. Cover with a tea towel and place in the fridge to marinate until you are ready to cook.

2. To make the Korean corn cheese, preheat the oven grill to high. Heat the olive oil in a large frying pan over medium–high heat, add the shallot and cook for 2–3 minutes until starting to soften. Add the corn kernels and cook for another 5–7 minutes until the corn is tender. Stir in the cayenne pepper and spring onion and cook for another minute. Transfer the corn mixture to a small baking dish. Mix through the feta, then flatten the mixture down and sprinkle the mozzarella over the top. Place under the grill for 3–5 minutes, until the top is golden brown. Remove and cover with foil to keep warm.

3. Place the frying pan back over medium–high heat. Add the olive oil and, once hot, add the marinated steaks and cook for 3 minutes each side for medium-rare, or until cooked to your liking. Remove to a plate and leave to rest while you cook the green beans.

4. Add the green beans to the pan and toss to coat in the residual oil. Cover with a lid and cook for 5–8 minutes, tossing only occasionally so they blister and char on the base of the pan.

5. Cut the steaks against the grain into thin slices and divide among four plates. Serve with the Korean corn cheese and blistered green beans.

Wholegrain high-fibre breads, cereals and legumes **0** ✳ Lean meat, fish, poultry, eggs, tofu and legumes **2** ✳ Fruit **0** ✳ Vegetables **2** ✳ Dairy **1** ✳ Healthy fats and oils **2.5**

Turkish kofta feast

16 g
TOTAL FIBRE

★★★
FIBRE RATING

1 tablespoon extra virgin olive oil

3 tablespoons pine nuts

1 large wholemeal pita bread, warmed and torn

1 bunch radishes, bulbs halved or quartered

3 Lebanese cucumbers, chopped

Baba ghanoush

2 large eggplants, halved lengthways

2 teaspoons extra virgin olive oil

2 garlic cloves, skin on

1 cup flat-leaf parsley leaves, roughly chopped

1 teaspoon ground cumin

1 teaspoon sweet paprika

juice of 1 lemon

Lamb koftas

750 g lean minced lamb

2 garlic cloves, minced

1 small onion, very finely diced or grated

1 cup flat-leaf parsley leaves, very finely chopped

1 free-range egg

2 teaspoons ground coriander

2 teaspoons ground cumin

1 teaspoon ground cinnamon

3 tablespoons wholemeal plain flour

¼ teaspoon freshly ground black pepper

1. Preheat the oven to 180°C (160°C fan-forced).
2. To make the baba ghanoush, place the eggplants, cut side up, on a baking tray and drizzle evenly with the olive oil. Add the garlic cloves to the tray, then place in the lower half of the oven and roast for 45 minutes, until the flesh is tender.
3. Meanwhile, to make the lamb koftas, place all the ingredients in a large bowl and mix really well with your hands until combined. Roll into small (about 3 cm) meatballs and place on a large baking tray. Place in the upper section of the oven and bake for 10 minutes, until their shape is set and they're starting to brown. Remove from the oven.
4. Heat the olive oil in a large frying pan over medium-high heat, add the meatballs in batches and cook for 2–3 minutes until nicely browned all over. Set aside and cover to keep warm.
5. Wipe out the excess oil and return the pan to medium heat. Add the pine nuts and cook, tossing, for 2–3 minutes until golden all over. Set aside for serving.
6. To finish the baba ghanoush, remove the eggplant from the oven and allow to cool slightly, then slice the nub off the end and roughly chop the eggplant (keeping the skin on for extra fibre). Strain excess liquid if necessary. Place in a food processor and squeeze in the roasted garlic flesh, discarding the skins. Add the remaining ingredients and blitz to form a smooth, but still slightly chunky paste (the skins won't completely blend, but don't worry, they taste great!). Scoop into a bowl to serve.
7. Arrange the kofta meatballs, baba ghanoush, toasted pine nuts, pita, radish and cucumber in the middle of the table and invite everyone to help themselves.

Wholegrain high-fibre breads, cereals and legumes 1 ✳ Lean meat, fish, poultry, eggs, tofu and legumes 2 ✳ Fruit 0 ✳ Vegetables 3 ✳ Dairy 0 ✳ Healthy fats and oils 3

Lamb cutlets with beetroot and cos salad

8g
TOTAL FIBRE

★★★
FIBRE RATING

4 beetroots, peeled and left whole

2 tablespoons white vinegar

800 g lean lamb cutlets on the bone, excess fat removed

2 tablespoons Dijon mustard

1 tablespoon extra virgin olive oil

Cos salad

1 cos lettuce, leaves roughly torn

2 Lebanese cucumbers, halved lengthways and thinly sliced into half moons

½ large avocado, flesh cut into 1 cm cubes

juice of ½ lemon

2 teaspoons extra virgin olive oil

80 g reduced-fat goat's feta, crumbled

2 tablespoons unsalted roasted almonds, roughly chopped

1. Preheat the oven to 180°C (160°C fan-forced).
2. Place each beetroot in a piece of foil and drizzle 2 teaspoons vinegar over each one. Wrap up in the foil, then place in the oven and roast for 1 hour, or until tender (the cooking time can vary depending on the size of the beetroot, so keep an eye on them).
3. Meanwhile, to make the cos salad, toss together all the ingredients in a large bowl. Set aside.
4. Place the lamb cutlets in a large bowl, add the mustard and a good grinding of black pepper. Massage the mustard into the cutlets until evenly coated.
5. Heat the olive oil in a large frying pan over medium–high heat. Once hot, add the cutlets and cook for 2–3 minutes each side or until cooked to your liking.
6. Remove the beetroots from the foil and cut into quarters. Divide the cutlets and beetroot among serving plates and serve with the cos salad.

TIP

Remember that the bones will add weight to the lamb cutlets. If buying lamb fillets without a bone, choose a lean cut and stick to a portion of 200 g per serve.

Wholegrain high-fibre breads, cereals and legumes **0** ✳ Lean meat, fish, poultry, eggs, tofu and legumes **2** ✳ Fruit **0** ✳ Vegetables **2** ✳ Dairy **0.5** ✳ Healthy fats and oils **3.5**

SERVES: 4   **PREP:** 20 MINS   **COOK:** 1 HOUR

Sweet potatoes with spiced lamb

17 g
TOTAL FIBRE

FIBRE RATING

RESISTANT STARCH

4 small sweet potatoes (600 g in total)

1 tablespoon extra virgin olive oil

600 g lean minced lamb

1 large red onion, diced

2 zucchini, diced

3 garlic cloves, minced

2 cups (320 g) cooked chickpeas (see pages 120–121)

2 teaspoons ground cumin

1 tablespoon ground coriander

1 teaspoon ground cinnamon

4 sprigs mint, leaves picked and finely chopped

3 tablespoons flat-leaf parsley leaves, finely chopped

⅓ cup (40 g) sliced unsalted roasted almonds

½ cup (125 g) reduced-fat Greek yoghurt

Green salad

2 Lebanese cucumbers, halved lengthways, thinly sliced into half moons

6 cups (120 g) mixed salad leaves

2 teaspoons extra virgin olive oil

juice of ½ lemon

60 g reduced-fat feta

1. Preheat the oven to 180°C (160°C fan-forced).
2. Place the whole sweet potatoes on a baking tray and drizzle over about 1 teaspoon of the olive oil, using your hands to coat them well. Place on the middle shelf of the oven and bake for 1 hour or until tender.
3. Meanwhile, heat 1 teaspoon of the olive oil in a large frying pan over medium heat. Add the lamb and cook for 10 minutes or until browned, breaking up any large lumps as you go. Add the onion, zucchini and remaining olive oil and cook for another 5 minutes until the veggies are tender. Add the garlic and chickpeas and cook for another minute until the garlic is fragrant. Add the ground spices and cook for 2 minutes until fragrant and well combined. Remove from the heat and cover to keep warm.
4. To make the green salad, place the cucumber and salad leaves in a large bowl. Drizzle over the olive oil and lemon juice and gently toss to coat well, then crumble over the feta.
5. Divide the baked sweet potatoes among serving plates and carefully slice down the middle, prying them open. Spoon on the lamb and chickpea mixture, top with the mint, parsley, almonds and a dollop of yoghurt and serve with the salad.

Wholegrain high-fibre breads, cereals and legumes **1** ✳ Lean meat, fish, poultry, eggs, tofu and legumes **2** ✳ Fruit **0** ✳ Vegetables **2** ✳ Dairy **0.5** ✳ Healthy fats and oils **3**

SNACKS

Popcorn

3g
TOTAL FIBRE

★
FIBRE RATING

Cheesy lemon popcorn

2 tablespoons extra virgin olive oil

⅓ cup (65 g) popcorn kernels

60 g parmesan, very finely grated

finely grated zest of 1 small lemon

1 teaspoon garlic powder

Heat 2 teaspoons of the olive oil in a large saucepan over high heat. Add the popcorn and cover, shaking the pan often to stop the kernels sticking to the bottom. When the popping slows to a few seconds between pops, remove from the heat and set aside until it stops completely.

Tip the popcorn into a large bowl. Sprinkle over the parmesan, lemon zest and garlic powder, drizzle over the remaining olive oil and toss until the popcorn is nicely coated.

Curried peanut popcorn

2 tablespoons extra virgin olive oil

⅓ cup (65 g) popcorn kernels

2 teaspoons curry powder

1½ tablespoons (15 g) unsalted roasted peanuts, very finely chopped

Follow the instructions for making the popcorn, left.

Tip the popcorn into a large bowl. Sprinkle over the curry powder and peanuts, drizzle over the remaining olive oil and toss until the popcorn is nicely coated. The peanuts should be chopped finely enough that they get stuck in the crevices of the popcorn, rather than falling to the bottom of the bowl.

Smoky paprika popcorn

2 tablespoons extra virgin olive oil

⅓ cup (65 g) popcorn kernels

1 tablespoon smoked paprika

finely grated zest of 1 lime

Follow the instructions for making the popcorn, left.

Tip the popcorn into a large bowl. Sprinkle over the paprika and lime zest, drizzle over the remaining olive oil and toss until the popcorn is nicely coated.

Wholegrain high-fibre breads, cereals and legumes 0.5 ✳
Dairy 0.5 ✳ Healthy fats and oils 2

Wholegrain high-fibre breads, cereals and legumes 0.5 ✳
Healthy fats and oils 3

Wholegrain high-fibre breads, cereals and legumes 0.5 ✳
Healthy fats and oils 4

Smoky paprika
popcorn

Curried peanut
popcorn

Cheesy lemon
popcorn

Cauliflower feta dip and seeded crackers

6g TOTAL FIBRE

★★ FIBRE RATING

½ head cauliflower, cut into florets

2 garlic cloves, skin on

2 teaspoons ground coriander

1½ tablespoons extra virgin olive oil

1 anchovy fillet

160 g reduced-fat goat's feta

½ cup (125 g) reduced-fat natural yoghurt

1 cup (160 g) cooked butter beans (see pages 120–121) or drained and rinsed tinned butter beans

juice of ½ lemon

1 tablespoon unsalted walnuts, crushed

4 cups mixed raw sliced vegetables (snow peas, radish, celery, carrot, capsicum or cucumber), to serve

Seeded crackers

90 g rolled oats

2 tablespoons flaxseeds

2 tablespoons pumpkin seeds (pepitas)

2 tablespoons sunflower seeds

2 tablespoons sesame seeds

1½ tablespoons poppy seeds

½ teaspoon fennel seeds, lightly crushed

2 tablespoons extra virgin olive oil

1. Preheat the oven to 180°C (160°C fan-forced).

2. To make the crackers, place the oats in a food processor or blender and blitz into small (1-2 mm) pieces. Add the flaxseeds and pumpkin seeds and pulse a few times until the pumpkin seeds are roughly chopped. Tip into a bowl, add the remaining ingredients and ½ cup (125 ml) water and mix until well combined. If you need more water to bring the dough together, add it 1 tablespoon at a time. Set the mixture aside for 20 minutes to firm up.

3. Meanwhile, make a start on the cauliflower feta dip. Place the cauliflower florets and garlic cloves on a large baking tray, sprinkle over the ground coriander and 1 tablespoon olive oil and toss to coat. Spread out over the tray and bake for 25 minutes, until the florets are tender and golden brown on the edges. Remove and set aside to cool, leaving the oven on for the crackers.

4. Place the cracker mixture between two sheets of baking paper. Using a rolling pin, roll it out to a 3–4 mm thickness (don't roll it too thin or the crackers will crumble when cooked). Remove the top layer of baking paper and slide the seed mix and bottom layer of paper onto a large baking tray.

Wholegrain high-fibre breads, cereals and legumes **0.5** ✳ Vegetables **1** ✳ Dairy **0.5** ✳ Healthy fats and oils **4**

5. Place in the oven and bake for 20 minutes, then remove and carefully flip the seed mixture over. If it cracks in places, don't worry – you'll be breaking it into crackers anyway! Bake for another 10 minutes until golden brown. Remove from the oven and cool for 10 minutes, before breaking into crackers.

6. To finish the dip, place the cooled cauliflower in a food processor and squeeze in the flesh from the garlic cloves. Add the anchovy, feta, yoghurt, butter beans and lemon juice and blitz to form a smooth paste. For a smoother consistency, add a dash of water and blitz again.

7. Scoop into a serving bowl and sprinkle over the walnuts. Finish with the remaining olive oil and a good grinding of black pepper.

8. Serve the dip with the seeded crackers and the raw vegetables.

TIPS

* Store the crackers in an airtight container for up to 1 week.
* The dip will keep in an airtight container in the fridge for up to 5 days.

Cauliflower feta
dip and seeded
crackers
PAGE 198

Roasted strawberries and ricotta

5g
TOTAL
FIBRE

★★
FIBRE
RATING

500 g strawberries, hulled and halved

2 teaspoons extra virgin olive oil

2 teaspoons vanilla extract

finely grated zest and juice of ½ lemon

3 tablespoons unsalted pistachio kernels, roughly chopped

2 cups (500 g) reduced-fat fresh ricotta

1. Preheat the oven to 180°C (160°C fan-forced) and line a large baking tray with baking paper.

2. Place the strawberries, olive oil, vanilla and lemon zest and juice on the prepared tray and toss together with your hands. Spread out in a single layer, then place in the oven and roast for 20–25 minutes until the strawberries are caramelised, but still holding their shape.

3. Meanwhile, heat a frying pan over medium heat and toast the chopped pistachios, tossing regularly, for 5 minutes or until golden.

4. Divide the ricotta among four bowls and spoon the roasted strawberries over the top. Finish with a sprinkling of pistachios and serve.

TIP

Swap the pistachios for unsalted cashews for extra resistant starch.

Fruit 1 ✳ Dairy 1 ✳ Healthy fats and oils **2.5**

Mushroom and goat's feta chickpea flatbread

5g TOTAL FIBRE   ★★ FIBRE RATING   ✓ RESISTANT STARCH

1 tablespoon extra virgin olive oil

1 small onion, thinly sliced

200 g brown mushrooms, sliced

1 garlic clove, minced

1 sprig rosemary, leaves picked

80 g reduced-fat goat's feta, crumbled

3 tablespoons walnuts, roughly chopped

2 tablespoons flat-leaf parsley leaves

freshly ground black pepper

Flatbread batter

90 g chickpea flour (besan)

1 tablespoon extra virgin olive oil

1. To make the batter, place the chickpea flour, olive oil and 1 cup (250 ml) water.
2. In a large bowl and whisk to form a smooth batter. Cover with a tea towel and rest for at least 30 minutes and up to 6 hours.
3. Heat the olive oil in a large frying pan over medium heat, add the onion, mushroom, garlic and rosemary and cook for 5–7 minutes until the mushroom and onion are tender and well cooked. Remove from the pan and set aside.
4. Preheat the oven grill to high.
5. Put the pan back over medium–high heat, pour in the batter and swirl to coat the base. Arrange the mushroom mixture, feta and walnuts on top, allowing them to sink into the batter. Cook for 4–5 minutes, until the bottom of the flatbread is set and golden brown when lifted with a spatula. Place under the grill for 3–5 minutes until the top of the flatbread is set.
6. Slide the flatbread onto a wooden board, sprinkle over the parsley and finish with a generous grinding of black pepper. Slice into triangles and serve.

Wholegrain high-fibre breads, cereals and legumes **0.5** ✳ Vegetables **0.5** ✳ Dairy **<0.5** ✳ Healthy fats and oils **2**

SERVES: 4   **PREP:** 15 MINS, PLUS SOAKING TIME   **COOK:** 25 MINS

Lentil pancakes

6g — TOTAL FIBRE   **★★** — FIBRE RATING   **√** — RESISTANT STARCH

1 cup (250 g) red lentils

2 tablespoons extra virgin olive oil

1 small onion, thinly sliced

1 small garlic clove, minced

1 small carrot, grated

½ teaspoon ground cumin

½ teaspoon ground coriander

¼ teaspoon ground turmeric

pinch of dried chilli flakes

¾ cup (185 g) reduced-fat natural yoghurt

2 tablespoons unsalted roasted almonds, finely chopped

herbs, to garnish

1. Soak the red lentils in a large bowl of water for 4–6 hours or overnight.

2. Heat 1 tablespoon olive oil in a frying pan over medium heat, add the onion and cook for 5 minutes or until translucent. Add the garlic, carrot, ground spices and chilli and cook for another minute or until fragrant.

3. Drain the lentils and place in a blender. Add 2 tablespoons water and blitz to form a thick, smooth paste. Add a dash more water if needed to bring the mixture together.

4. Tip the lentil paste into a large bowl and stir through the cooked onion mixture and a big pinch of freshly ground black pepper.

5. Return the frying pan to medium heat and heat the remaining olive oil. Working in two batches of four, add 3 tablespoons lentil mixture per pancake and cook for 3–4 minutes each side until golden brown.

6. Place two pancakes on each serving plate and finish with a dollop of yoghurt, herbs, almonds and a good grinding of black pepper.

Wholegrain high-fibre breads, cereals and legumes **0.5** ✳ Vegetables **0.5** ✳ Dairy **<0.5** ✳ Healthy fats and oils **3**

Edamame

Garlic sesame edamame

SERVES: 4 **PREP:** 5 MINS **COOK:** 10 MINS

TOTAL FIBRE   FIBRE RATING

2 cups (200 g) frozen edamame in pods
2 tablespoons extra virgin olive oil
1 tablespoon sesame seeds
2 garlic cloves, minced
2 teaspoons sesame oil

Boil the edamame according to the packet instructions, then drain.

Heat the olive oil in a large frying pan over medium heat. Add the sesame seeds and garlic and cook, stirring, for 2–3 minutes, until the seeds are golden and the garlic is fragrant. Add the edamame and sesame oil and toss to coat well. Serve warm.

Chilli peanut edamame

SERVES: 4 **PREP:** 5 MINS **COOK:** 10 MINS

TOTAL FIBRE   FIBRE RATING

2 cups (200 g) frozen edamame in pods
2½ tablespoons extra virgin olive oil
1 golden shallot, halved and thinly sliced
pinch of dried chilli flakes
1 tablespoon unsalted roasted peanuts, finely chopped

Cook the edamame according to the packet instructions. Drain and set aside.

Heat the olive oil in a large frying pan over medium heat, add the shallot and cook for 4 minutes until softened and lightly golden. Add the chilli flakes and peanuts and stir for another 1–2 minutes until the peanuts are golden and the chilli is fragrant. Add the edamame and toss to coat in the spiced oil. Serve warm.

Vegetables **0.5** ✳ Healthy fats and oils **2.5**

Vegetables **0.5** ✳ Healthy fats and oils **3**

Garlic sesame
edamame

Chilli peanut
edamame

Froyo bites

3g
TOTAL
FIBRE

★
FIBRE
RATING

1 cup (250 g) reduced-fat natural yoghurt

250 g fresh or frozen strawberries, hulled

juice of ½ lemon

3 tablespoons cashew butter (or any nut butter)

3 tablespoons coconut flakes

1. Place the yoghurt, strawberries, lemon juice and cashew butter in a blender and blend until smooth. Stir through the coconut flakes.

2. Spoon the mixture into the holes of an ice-cube tray (preferably with large square holes). Freeze for at least 6 hours or overnight until frozen.

Fruit **0.5** ✳ Dairy **0.5** ✳ Healthy fats and oils **3.5**

SERVES: 4   **PREP:** 10 MINS

Apple slices with almond butter 'frosting'

4g
TOTAL FIBRE

★★
FIBRE RATING

3 tablespoons almond butter
(or cashew or peanut butter)

1 teaspoon tapioca flour

1 teaspoon vanilla extract

¼ teaspoon ground cinnamon

2–3 tablespoons skim milk

2 medium red apples, cored and
sliced into 5 mm thick rings

2 teaspoons desiccated coconut

1. Mix together the nut butter, tapioca flour, vanilla and cinnamon in a bowl. Add 2 tablespoons of the milk and stir to combine, adding a little more if needed to loosen up the mixture.

2. 'Frost' each apple ring with the nut butter mixture, then sprinkle over the desiccated coconut to look like icing sugar.

Wholegrain high fibre breads, cereals and legumes **<0.5** ✳ Fruit **0.5** ✳ Dairy **<0.5** ✳ Healthy fats and oils **4**

Berry overload banana muffins

3g
TOTAL FIBRE

★
FIBRE RATING

2 medium ripe bananas

⅓ cup (80 ml) olive oil

½ cup (125 g) reduced-fat natural yoghurt or plant-based yoghurt

3 large free-range eggs

2 teaspoons vanilla extract

1 cup (125 g) green banana flour

½ cup (55 g) almond meal

½ cup (50 g) rolled oats

2 teaspoons baking powder

3 tablespoons shredded coconut

1 cup (125 g) fresh or frozen raspberries

1. Preheat the oven to 180°C (160°C fan-forced) and line a 12-hole muffin tin with paper cases.
2. Mash the bananas to a puree in a large bowl. Add the olive oil, yoghurt, eggs and vanilla extract and whisk together with a fork. Add the flour, almond meal, oats, baking powder and 2 tablespoons of the shredded coconut and mix to form a smooth batter. Gently fold in most of the raspberries, reserving a few for garnish.
3. Divide the mixture evenly among the muffin holes, then sprinkle over the remaining shredded coconut and gently push in the reserved raspberries. Bake for 20–25 minutes, or until golden and a skewer inserted in the centre of a muffin comes out clean.
4. Cool in the tin for a few minutes, then transfer to a wire rack to cool completely.

TIP

These muffins freeze well. Wrap them up separately and store in the freezer for up to 3 months. Thaw in the fridge overnight, then reheat in the microwave or in a moderate oven.

Wholegrain high-fibre breads, cereals and legumes **0.5** ✳ Lean meat, fish, poultry, eggs, tofu and legumes **<0.5** ✳ Fruit **0.5** ✳ Dairy **<0.5** ✳ Healthy fats and oils **2**

Banana bowls

5g
TOTAL
FIBRE

★★
FIBRE
RATING

✓
RESISTANT
STARCH

2 tablespoons unsalted macadamias, roughly chopped

3 cups (750 g) reduced-fat natural yoghurt

2 large bananas, sliced

2 mangoes, cheeks sliced into 2 cm cubes

2 teaspoons chia seeds

1 tablespoon peanut butter (no added sugar or salt)

pinch of ground cinnamon, to garnish

1. Heat a frying pan over medium heat, add the macadamias and cook, tossing, for 2–3 minutes until toasted and golden.
2. Divide the yoghurt among four bowls. Top with the banana, mango, macadamias, chia seeds and peanut butter. Sprinkle over a dusting of cinnamon and serve.

Fruit 1 ✳ Dairy 1 ✳ Healthy fats and oils **2**

TIP

Use slightly under-ripe (green) bananas and unsalted cashews instead of the macadamias for extra resistant starch.

SERVES: 2   **PREP:** 5 MINS   **COOK:** 2 MINS

5 g
TOTAL
FIBRE

★★
FIBRE
RATING

✓
RESISTANT
STARCH

Chocolate mug cake

1 small banana

3 tablespoons quinoa flakes

1 small free-range egg

2 tablespoons unsweetened cocoa powder

½ teaspoon baking powder

2 teaspoons milk

½ teaspoon vanilla extract

1 tablespoon nut butter (almond, peanut or cashew)

pinch of ground cinnamon, plus extra to serve

1. In a bowl, mash the banana with the back of a fork. Add the quinoa flakes, egg, cocoa powder, baking powder, milk and vanilla and mix to form a thick batter.
2. Divide the batter between two mugs. Microwave separately for 1 minute on high.
3. Serve warm with nut butter and an extra pinch of cinnamon.

Wholegrain high-fibre breads, cereals and legumes **0.5** ✻ Lean meat, fish, poultry, eggs, tofu and legumes **<0.5** ✻ Fruit **0.5** ✻ Dairy **<0.5** ✻ Healthy fats and oils **2**

REFERENCES

Bird AR, Conlon MA, Christophersen CT and Topping DL (2010). 'Resistant starch, large bowel fermentation and a broader perspective of prebiotics.' *Beneficial Microbes* 1: 423-431.

Choo JM, Tran CD, Luscombe-Marsh ND, Stonehouse W, Bowen J, Johnson N, Thompson CH, Watson EJ, Brinkworth GD, Rogers GB (2020). 'Almond consumption affects fecal microbiota composition, stool pH, and stool moisture in overweight and obese adults with elevated fasting blood glucose: a randomised controlled trial.' *Nutr Res.* 2021;85:47-59. doi: 10.1016/j.nutres.2020.11.005.

Conlon MA and Bird AR (2015). 'The impact of diet and lifestyle on gut microbiota and human health.' *Nutrients* 7:17-44.

Costello SP, Hughes PA, Waters O, Bryant RV, Vincent AD, Blatchford P, Katsikeros R, Makanyanga J, Campaniello MA, Mavrangelos C, Rosewarne CP, Bickley C, Peters C, Schoeman MN, Conlon MA, Roberts-Thomson IC, Andrews JM (2019). 'Effect of fecal microbiota transplantation on 8-week remission in patients with ulcerative colitis: a randomised clinical trial.' *JAMA* 321:156-164.

Harbison JE, Roth-Schulze AJ, Giles LC, Tran CD, Ngui KM, Penno MA, Thomson RL, Wentworth JM, Colman PG, Craig ME, Morahan G, Papenfuss AT, Barry SC, Harrison LC, Couper JJ (2019). 'Gut microbiome dysbiosis and increased intestinal permeability in children with islet autoimmunity and type 1 diabetes: a prospective cohort study.' *Pediatr Diabetes.* 2019;20(5):574-583. doi: 10.1111/pedi.12865.

Harbison JE, Thomson RL, Wentworth JM, Louise J, Roth-Schulze A, Battersby RJ, Ngui KM, Penno MAS, Colman PG, Craig ME, Barry SC, Tran CD, Makrides M, Harrison LC, Couper JJ (2021). 'Associations between diet, the gut microbiome and short chain fatty acids in youth with islet autoimmunity and type 1 diabetes.' *Pediatr Diabetes.* 2021;22(3):425-433. doi: 10.1111/pedi.13178

Kerr CA, Grice DM, Tran CD, Bauer DC, Li D, Hendry P, Hannan GN (2015). 'Early life events influence whole-of-life metabolic health via gut microflora and gut permeability.' *Crit Rev Microbiol.* 2015;41(3):326-40. doi: 10.3109/1040841X.2013.837863.

Le Leu RK, Winter J, Humphreys K, Young GP, Christophersen CT, Hu Y, Gratz SW, Miller RB, Topping DL, Bird AR and Conlon MA (2015). 'Effects of red meat and butyrylated resistant starch on rectal 06-methyl-guanine adducts, microbiota and biochemical biomarkers of colorectal cancer risk: a randomised clinical trial.' *British Journal of Nutrition* 114:220-230.

McOrist AL, Miller RB, Bird AR, Keogh JB, Noakes M, Topping DL and Conlon MA (2011). 'Fecal butyrate levels vary widely among individuals but are usually increased by a diet high in resistant starch.' *Journal of Nutrition* 141: 883-889.

Tran CD, Grice DM, Wade B, Kerr CA, Bauer DC, Li D, Hannan GN (2015). 'Gut permeability, its interaction with gut microflora and effects on metabolic health are mediated by the lymphatics system, liver and bile acid.' *Future Microbiol.* 2015;10(8):1339-53. doi: 10.2217/FMB.15.54.

Vuillermin PJ, O'Hely P, Collier F, Allen KJ, Tang MLK, Harrison LC, Carlin JB, Saffery R, Ranganathan S, Sly PD, Gray L, Molloy J, Pezic A, Conlon M, Topping D, Nelson K, Mackay CR, Macia L, Koplin J, Dawson SL, Moreno-Betancur M, Ponsonby A-L, the J. Craig Venter Institute, the BIS Investigator Group (2020). 'Maternal carriage of Prevotella during pregnancy associates with protection against food allergy in the offspring.' *Nature Communications* 11:1452.

Weersma RK, Zhernokova A and Fu J (2020). 'Interaction betwen drugs and the gut microbiome.' *Gut*, 2020; 0:1-10. doi: 10.1136/gutjnl-2019-320204

BRISTOL STOOL CHART

	Type 1	Separate hard lumps	Severe constipation
	Type 2	Lumpy and sausage like	Mild constipation
	Type 3	A sausage shape with cracks in the surface	Normal
	Type 4	Like a smooth, soft sausage or snake	Normal
	Type 5	Soft blobs with clear-cut edges	Lacking fibre
	Type 6	Mushy consistency with ragged edges	Mild diarrhoea
	Type 7	Liquid consistency with no solid pieces	Severe diarrhoea

Conversion chart

Measuring cups and spoons may vary slightly from one country to another, but the difference is generally not enough to affect a recipe. All cup and spoon measures are level.

One Australian metric measuring cup holds 250 ml (8 fl oz), one Australian tablespoon holds 20 ml (4 teaspoons) and one Australian metric teaspoon holds 5 ml. North America, New Zealand and the UK use a 15 ml (3-teaspoon) tablespoon.

Length

Metric	Imperial
3 mm	⅛ inch
6 mm	¼ inch
1 cm	½ inch
2.5 cm	1 inch
5 cm	2 inches
18 cm	7 inches
20 cm	8 inches
23 cm	9 inches
25 cm	10 inches
30 cm	12 inches

Liquid measures

One American pint	One Imperial pint
500 ml (16 fl oz)	600 ml (20 fl oz)

Cup	Metric	Imperial
⅛ cup	30 ml	1 fl oz
¼ cup	60 ml	2 fl oz
⅓ cup	80 ml	2½ fl oz
½ cup	125 ml	4 fl oz
⅔ cup	160 ml	5 fl oz
¾ cup	180 ml	6 fl oz
1 cup	250 ml	8 fl oz
2 cups	500 ml	16 fl oz
2¼ cups	560 ml	20 fl oz
4 cups	1 litre	32 fl oz

Dry measures

The most accurate way to measure dry ingredients is to weigh them. However, if using a cup, add the ingredient loosely to the cup and level with a knife; don't compact the ingredient unless the recipe requests 'firmly packed'.

Metric	Imperial
15 g	½ oz
30 g	1 oz
60 g	2 oz
125 g	4 oz (¼ lb)
185 g	6 oz
250 g	8 oz (½ lb)
375 g	12 oz (¾ lb)
500 g	16 oz (1 lb)
1 kg	32 oz (2 lb)

Oven temperatures

Celsius	Fahrenheit
100°C	200°F
120°C	250°F
150°C	300°F
160°C	325°F
180°C	350°F
200°C	400°F
220°C	425°F

Celsius	Gas mark
110°C	¼
130°C	½
140°C	1
150°C	2
170°C	3
180°C	4
190°C	5
200°C	6
220°C	7
230°C	8
240°C	9
250°C	10

ACKNOWLEDGEMENTS

It is with great respect that we would like to thank past CSIRO scientists and thought leaders who have paved the way for the current authorship team. We therefore thank: Professor David Topping, Dr Trevor Lockett, Dr Julie Clark and Dr Tony Bird.

Our books always undergo internal and external reviews and for this we would like to thank Professor Gordon Howarth, Gastroeneterology Department of Women's and Children's Hospital; Dr Rosemary Stanton OAM, leading nutritionist and dietitian and visiting fellow at the school of medical sciences at University of NSW; Nick Wray, Senior Gastroenterology Dietitian and Director of 360Me Nutrition; and Dr Dep Huynh, Consultant Gastrointestinal and Hepatologist at the Queen Elizabeth Hospital, Adelaide.

We also thank individuals from CSIRO health and biosecurity for providing their professional expertise in reviewing the current content: Professor Bev Muhlhausler; Professor Grant Brinkworth; Dr Damien Belobradjdic; and all those who work tirelessly in our labs and clinical research teams to conduct the research that underpins the science you see translated into our publications: we can not do our science without you.

We would also like to thank the many science leaders and collaborators of our research, those in the past and those who continue to explore the diverse area of dietary intake and gut health. We understand that we have come a long way in this area of science, but we are excited by the future learnings we are about to embrace.

A thank you is extended to the incredibly talented publishing and editorial team at Pan Macmillian Australia: Ingrid Ohlsson, Ariane Durkin, Naomi van Groll, Sally Devenish, Clare Keighery, Adrik Kemp, Katri Hilden and Rachel Carter, as well as designer Jacqui Porter. The work here enables our complex scientific messages to be conveyed in simple, practical and visual terms for our readers. This content wouldn't be complete without incredible recipes, developed and tested by the talented Meg Yonson, photographed by Rob Palmer, prepped by Kerrie Ray and styled by Emma Knowles.

Finally, we are always interested in what you, our readers, tell us, so to all of you who contact us with your feedback and comments: thank you.

INDEX

First published 2021 in Macmillan
by Pan Macmillan Australia Pty Limited
1 Market Street, Sydney, New South Wales
Australia 2000

Text copyright © CSIRO 2021
Photography Rob Palmer copyright © Pan Macmillan 2021
Portrait photography on pages 4–11 © CSIRO; images on pages 23, 25, 27, 34, 85, 98 and 101 © Shutterstock; pages 29, 33-34 and 110-111 © Unsplash; page 32 © 123RF; page 79 © Charlotte May / Pexels; pages 67 and 109 © iStock

A catalogue record for this book is available from the National Library of Australia

NATIONAL LIBRARY OF AUSTRALIA

Design by Northwood Green
Recipe development by Meg Yonson
Prop and food styling by Emma Knowles
Food preparation by Kerrie Ray
Editing by Katri Hilden and Rachel Carter
Index by Jenny Browne

Colour + reproduction by Splitting Image Colour Studio
Printed in China by 1010 Printing International Limited

10 9 8 7 6 5 4 3 2 1